# Lean Problem Solving and QC Tools for Industrial Engineers

# Lean Problem Solving and QC Tools for Industrial Engineers

By

MAHARSHI SAMANTA

CRC Press
Taylor & Francis Group
Boca Raton London New York

CRC Press is an imprint of the
Taylor & Francis Group, an **informa** business

CRC Press
Taylor & Francis Group
6000 Broken Sound Parkway NW, Suite 300
Boca Raton, FL 3487-2742

First issued in paperback 2020

ISBN 13: 978-0-367-73004-8 (pbk)
ISBN 13: 978-1-138-33849-4 (hbk)

---

### Library of Congress Cataloging-in-Publication Data

---

Library of Congress Cataloging-in-Publication Data
Names: Samanta, Maharshi, author.
Title: Lean problem solving and QC tools for industrial engineers / Maharshi Samanta.
Description: First edition. | New York, NY : Taylor & Francis Group, 2019. | Includes bibliographical references and index.
Identifiers: LCCN 2018044843| ISBN 9781138338494 (hardback : acid-free paper) | ISBN 9780429441707 (ebook)
Subjects: LCSH: Quality control. | Lean manufacturing. | Problem solving.
Classification: LCC TS156 .S266 2019 | DDC 658.5/62–dc23
LC record available at https://lccn.loc.gov/2018044843

---

**Visit the Taylor & Francis Web site at**
http://www.taylorandfrancis.com

**and the CRC Press Web site at**
http://www.crcpress.com

*To the tireless, frontline, shop-floor managers and natural
team leaders in the manufacturing and service industries who
taught me the fundamentals of lean problem-solving.*

*To my mom, Mrs Mridula Samanta, who persisted till the end, and to my dad, Late
Dr. Gajendra Nath Samanta, who would have been very pleased with the outcome
of this effort. To my daughter, Roupkatha, for life's ultimate problem-solving.*

*And to our eventful journey of life that teaches us wisdom beyond
intellect. That wisdom makes us what we are today.*

# WHAT IS A PROBLEM?

# Contents

# *Preface*

Now more people are doing work that requires individual decisionmaking and problem-solving, and we need an educational system that will help develop these skills.

**Seymour Papert**

Way back in early 1990s, when I first started my journey as Product Installation and Sales Engineer, little did I know that slowly over a period of time the success philosophy of a person's entire lifetime can be really summarized to successful implementation of various concepts of problem-solving.

Later, throughout my engineering professional work, I received enriching experience in different fields, such as, Quality Control & Assurance, Production, Production Planning, Development, and Projects as diversified as manufacturing steel in integrated steel plants, manufacturing glass for cockpit displays to manufacturing very large screen plasma displays, where all the beautiful facets of physics, chemistry, material science and mathematics converged.

During this working tenure, I was fortunate to have experienced world class manufacturing practices, more specifically in organization-wide Six Sigma drive, continuous improvement methodologies. From the early stage of engagement, I found that at the heart of successful operation and impressive atmosphere of continuous improvement, there lies an unfailing effort of the team-leaders to do problem-solving at every conceivable area with whatever minimum resources available. I call this lean problem-solving. I always observed that this lean problem-solving drives through the DNA of an organization and create the all powerful atmosphere of continuous improvement and business excellence.

While working with multi cultural and multi domain teams, I observed that while problem-solving is the most sought after skill, it is one of the highly neglected skills in traditional university curriculum and in industrial practices as well. Therefore, a need is felt to document all the necessary facets of this important domain of skill-set.

This book is conceived and designed to help professionals in different fields, such as engineers, doctors, teachers, and research scholars alike, who face the regular challenge of developing and improving the status quo by solving problems in all spheres of their work. I frequently meet different sets of people in daily life who are working at various places. While professionals and engineers are challenging their individual skills to make their organization *lean,* doctors and teachers are challenging their knowledge to delve into a patient's heart or a student's head. These individuals share their problems and their life experiences with me. While serving as their consultant and counselor, I realized that when facing problems, we usually deal with a kind of policy paralysis and do not find a suitable way out. As a result, making a good decision remains pending, or even when a decision is made, it is not good enough. Therefore, the situation does not improve. After lingering within the process of improvement for some time, we eventually lose valuable time, money, and energy. After even more time, the situation no longer remains an individual's personal problem, it transforms into a critical point for a larger group. This is where knowledge of the art of problem-solving becomes more important and very useful.

In this book, an effort is made to communicate the ideas of problem-solving in an easy and comprehensible language. The ideas presented here will be helpful to one and all experienced professionals practicing in an otherwise lean business environment. Also an effort is made here to explain the concepts of problem-solving to those who are pursuing their undergraduate studies or to individuals who are comparatively new in their field of work. Needless to say, the fundamental concepts explained here are timeless. Therefore, these concepts will remain a source of knowledge and inspiration for juniors and seniors alike. Moreover, the skills for solving problems in an industrial setup can reduce the employability gap between employers' needs and employees' skills. Irrespective of whether a problem is a professional or a personal one, the acquired skill of problem-solving modifies as well as reflects upon the personal character of an individual. The learning experience thus gained defines a new attitude in those practicing these skills who start thinking in a very systematic manner. In other words, these skills bring out the true professional in an individual.

In general the entire concept dealt in this book is presented in three main parts. The Part I, explained in Chapters 1, 2, & 3, deals with the concept introduction and the general philosophy. In this part, I presented the definitions, various terms, challenges and opportunities available with the problem-solver. Very useful tips are also provided for achieving fairly good results in problem-solving. In addition to that with the aid of examples, characteristics of variations that give rise to problem-solving, the potential solution mechanism and the underlying philosophy is explained.

In Part II, I explained the fundamental steps of problem-solving. In addition the concepts of root cause analysis, Poka-Yoke techniques, and various other concepts are detailed for implementation of the solution, such as action plans and their standardization, monitoring and follow up for sustenance.

In Part III, comprising the chapters 6, 7 & 8, various techniques are explained for generating ideas and organizing the basic information, collecting data and collating information, systematic analysis, implementation of the solution and change management.

This book is written based on vast experience with real-time problem-solving techniques, especially in an industrial atmosphere. Every concept explained is supported by real-time examples from the lean practical world. These examples should make this book more interesting for professionals, teachers, and students alike. Also utmost care has been taken when choosing these examples so as to make the book more meaningful and lucid to thoughtful readers like you.

Understanding the fundamentals of the problem-solving may help you resolve issues not only in industrial manufacturing and service sector, but also in daily life. These ideas can inspire and motivate you to follow a methodical approach in everything you do.

# Acknowledgments

Acceptance of the truth or existence of something.

This book is the product of twenty-five years of study of various facets of problem-solving. Long ago, during the birth of a student in engineering, there were many a mentors. The long list starts with the great Chanakya Kautilya, the author of *Arthashastra* (Book of Economics), the great strategist philosopher of ancient India to Dr. W. Edwards Deming, the modern day quality guru. Thanks to the mantras they have taught through their timeless classics. This book may allow me to bring parity to the learning trade-imbalance that exists in favor of these stalwarts who have penned masterpieces for the use of professionals in the field of economics to operational excellence in manufacturing and service sector.

Throughout my working tenure, I have been also personally benefitted by many of my teachers, coworkers, and family members. Unfortunately, the names are so numerous that it is not possible to list them all. However, quite a few personalities have helped me learn the finer details of the subject we are dealing here. It will be a serious mistake on my part not to mention them here.

My sincere thanks to all those who have taken the time out to read my drafts of this book. I wish to express my appreciation for many helpful comments, suggestions and criticisms. They have suggested many changes that helped me refine the content and the delivery of the subject. These changes made the book more relevant and useful. My thanks goes to Dr. Anand Srivastava, Dr. Rajesh Tyagi, Dr. Muralidhar, Dr. Sharmaand, Dr. Harish K. Dwivedi, Dr. Rituporno Sen and Dr. Saikat Maitra.

Special thanks goes to Debjani Sarkar, Dr. Rajarshi Samanta, Dr. Muhammad Azeem Ashraf, and Dr. Erick C. Jones and Mr. C.N. Prasanna Kumar for providing critical analysis of the subject matter and their suggestions. All advice was incorporated to enrich the content.

Special thanks also goes to Umang Verma and Gajendra S Chouhan for helping me with the freehand illustrations and Manas Kumar Manna, Debjit Sarkar and Gauri Sarkar for all the enumerable mini suggestions and moral support.

I sincerely thank Ms. Victoria Jones for her thorough copy editing. Without her inputs this book would not have been what it is today.

My gratitude also goes to the publishing team who, despite all odds, made this book possible: Ms. Mouli Sharma, Dr. Gagandeep Singh, Ms. Jennifer Stair of CRC, and Ms. Kritika Kaushik and Ms. Apoorva Mathur of Cenveo Publisher Services. It has been fun working with you all! I hope that I did not drive you all too crazy with missed deadlines and frequent requests for changes in text!

# About the Author

**Maharshi Samanta** is a seasoned Six Sigma professional, a prolific speaker, and an unbound thinker in the corporate world. He earned his master's degree in chemical technology and devoted his working life to many facets of engineering—from manufacturing viewing windows for atomic reactors and displays for Mach 2 fighter jets to pioneering development work in the field of plasma displays. He presented several scientific and technological papers at international forums and patented several of his breakthrough inventions.

An alumnus of the Indian Institute of Management Calcutta and a visionary leader in manufacturing, he is highly skilled in lean operations, management by quality, organizational behavior, and strategy for top- and bottom-line growth. He is immersed in the field of world-class manufacturing concepts and lives the life of an ascetic daily problem-solver.

As an avid reader and adroit writer, he appeals directly to his disciples' minds with down-to-earth language and witty anecdotes. In this book, a consummate soccer player drives straight into the heartland of industrial problem-solving toward a lean organizational setup.

# 1

## Read Me First

You can't teach problem-solving unless you are a problem-solver.

**Jim Wilson**

## Objectives

After going through this chapter and understanding the issues described in it, you will be able to deal more efficiently with the challenges in industrial problem-solving:

1. *Explain* the characteristics of the problem-solving journey.
2. *Understand* the major dimensions of a problem and its impact on the problem–solution ecosystem.

3. *Identify* the reasons why people fail to solve problems.
4. *Recognize* the true path for a rewarding problem-solving journey.

## The Scenario

In our everyday life, we come across many situations where we find ourselves surrounded by chaos, which does not allow us to achieve the desired results; eventually, we refer to this chaos as a problem. However, the situation becomes more adverse when we do not find solutions to those problems, even after repeated trials. In the end, we find an unsuitable solution or an alternative in absence of a solution, or we abandon the project altogether. This perhaps is true for all of us in various professions, be they medical practices, engineering systems, bio-technological endeavors or any other walks of life. However different those professions may seem to be, though, at the core of it, all are of a similar nature in that there lies a gap between the desired results and the ongoing situations; this gap remains fundamental to a problem situation.

The closer the situation is to the desired condition, the better the quality of goods and services provided. The converse is also true, which indicates that the farther we are from the desired state of results, the worse results may be in terms of quality, service, and delivery. What defines the gap between these desired results and the present offering is some kind of problem that has not been resolved in the due course of time. This makes an assertion that the problem-solving isn't difficult. We just have to remember to do it. This also indicates that the problem is not understood properly, not attended thoroughly, or not resolved by following a systemic problem-solving journey.

---

"Problem-solving isn't difficult. We just have to remember to do it."

---

Here it may be noted that, in spite of all the similarities and dissimilarities, all problem-solving journeys have a few characteristics that are common to all. These characteristics can be summarized as follows.

- *Uncertainty of results:* Even when only probable actions are taken, the results always remain uncertain.
- *Objectivism:* Actions taken in a problem-solving project do have a desired end result at the end of a time line.

- *Uniqueness:* Every problem is unique, regardless of similarities they might have to other problems.
- *Cross-functional:* Every problem-solving technique requires the problem-solver to work with cross-functional aptitude to embody the skills and resources of various teams and individuals.

In addition to these characteristics, there are three major dimensions that govern the problem-solving journey. These are the scope of the problem, the time available for solving the problem, and the cost associated with it.

"Uniqueness of a problem, coupled with profound objectivism and uncertainty of results, makes a cross-functional team deliver astonishing results."

These three dimensions also are interlinked in such a way that any change in one will also affect the other two. If the scope increases, widens, or becomes more challenging, there is a possibility that both the associated cost and the time required for problem-solving will increase. Similarly, on the other hand, the associated cost may reduce as the losses reduce during the time. This essentially means that solving a problem requires us to achieve the specific goals within the scheduled time and budgeted cost.

Therefore, it can be empirically represented that

$$\text{Success}_{(\text{Problem-Solving})} = f(\text{Skill}) + f(\text{Cost, Scope, Time})$$

The associated cost here can be of two types—for example, the (invested) cost of solving a problem and the (incurred) cost of not solving a problem— that is the cost incurred for the loss of quality in a product or service. In this context, we also need to understand more about the concept of cost of quality. This will be discussed in subsequent sections.

### CRITICAL THINKING EXERCISE

Write the details about an industrial operational problem wherein success in resolving it greatly depends on skill, cost, scope, and time. Assign numbers to each of these aspects for their relative importance and try to arrive at an empirical formula to define success. Can you think of any other aspects besides these four?

## The Approach in This Book

In this book, utmost care is taken in elaborating the concept of problem-solving. The concept of problem-solving is considered holistically and, for the benefit of the average reader, a generalist approach is maintained throughout. The entire cycle of problem-solving is subdivided into a few easily understood sections, and these sections are treated in detail.

In reading this book, one will not require much prior knowledge to comprehend the ideas enumerated. The scientific concepts and technical background are introduced and analyzed in the course of discussion.

"In industrial problem-solving, a well-trained logical mind will not require much prior knowledge in the core subject."

However, in order to reduce the volume of this book and to keep the reader attentive throughout the reading experience, the sections are kept brief and simple. Advanced readers will find several references that they can use for supplementary reading.

### PROBLEMS ARE GREAT TEACHERS

## Who Should Read This Book

This book is written for all people with logical minds who want to bring in a systematic process approach toward solving a problem. It is intended for working professionals and students alike in the field of industrial manufacturing, industrial service, industrial psychology, and those in various other fields of interest.

Though the word QUALITY refers to the quality of an industrially manufactured product or service, the reference in this book does not restrict itself only to this laconic meaning.

A doctor, a lawyer, a veterinarian, or even a teacher will benefit equally by applying the approach illustrated here.

This book will be a ready reference for practicing managers and natural team leaders to apply the concepts in their daily work lives and also to coach their team members. A person scheduled to appear for a job interview will find it handy for a technical session.

Engineering students and those in other professions should review this book and try to implement the ideas presented not only in their professional spheres but also in their personal lives.

## FAILURES IN PROBLEM-SOLVING.

**WHY PEOPLE FAIL TO SOLVE PROBLEMS**

**BECOME** EASY PREY TO **EARLY WARNING** SIGNS.
TENDENCY TO JUMP INTO A SOLUTION.
**RELUCTANT** TO BE DISCIPLINED.
ACTING WITHOUT A CONSENSUS.
LACK OF UNDERSTANDING.
TREATING THE SYMPTOMS.
LACK OF PATIENCE.

## What This Book Will Bring to the Reader's Mind

This book is designed to enlighten a logical mind to think in a systematic manner toward resolving a problem. Reading the examples will create a practical foundation for structured problem analysis.

A wise man once said that an experience is not how many years you work, but what you learn from what you do. It is needless to say that while you work for something, you may either succeed or not succeed in achieving results. And you will agree that in both cases, the learning—and therefore the resulting experience—will differ greatly. It may be that what is learned while *not* achieving results or objectives far outshines that which is learned while achieving results or objectives.

> "Experience is not what you did but what you learned from what you did."

Therefore, the concept of "experience" as explained in the first instance may be further modified to illustrate that experience is what someone learns when they do not achieve the desired end results. Thus, to some extent, the experience is a manifestation of failure that bears fruit as learning.

This book is testimony to lengthy implementation of real-time problem-solving while experiencing repeated failure. It is therefore of utmost importance to share a few highlights that will help readers form the basis for systematic thinking.

It is overly simplistic to say that a system approach will allow an otherwise average individual to excel in life. This in turn will help the reader not forget any vital steps.

> "Learning while not achieving results or objectives far outshines the learning while achieving results and objectives."

The approach in this book focus on the real issues and not red herrings. It will also help individuals to differentiate between a vital few problems or solutions and many trivial possibilities. This is of real benefit in time-stressed situations.

## Why Do People Fail to Solve Problems?

With the best of intentions, everybody wants to reduce problems in hand by solving them. However, many times people fail to solve a problem. While there can be several reasons for failure, a few critically important reasons are enumerated here [1].

a. **Lack of understanding** about the gravity of the solution may become a hindrance. Sometimes the solutions are so idealistic in nature that implementation remains a tough call, and the solutions remain unachieved.

b. **Reluctance to understand** the short-term and long-term side effects of the measures taken to resolve a problem may seriously shorten the success rate of an action taken. To obtain the desired results, one has to endure the onslaught of the side effects.

c. **A reluctance to be disciplined** but having wisdom enough to follow a systematic procedure may lead one to erratic correlation of the data set.

d. **Lack of patience** in collecting sufficient data to help analyze the problem may result in an inability to see the whole picture. Further analysis then becomes erroneous.

e. **Falling prey to early indications** that a problem is solved occurs when one gets first results fast—very fast. One becomes content before getting the full results and thereby loses perspective in the long run.

f. **An inherent tendency to jump into a solution** is perhaps the worst of the mistakes one can make. One does not weigh all the options and does not see the whole picture. This leads to improper goal setting, eventual failure, and even a false sense of achievement.

g. **Treating the symptoms instead of a root cause** will eventually lead to nowhere. A better approach would be to search and find the root cause and then systematically find the solution.

h. **Acting without a consensus** and a clear goal among the team members may result in an improper objective orientation and lack of team support while implementing an otherwise great solution mechanism.

## CRITICAL THINKING EXERCISE

Pause for a moment and think for a while. Describe a situation from your life's experience where lack of patience and jumping into untested solutions potentially may end an otherwise very prospective[1] problem-solving journey.

Make a list of various aspects why you think that our present failure propositions might be really true.

---

[1] Expected or expecting to become a specified thing in the future.

UNDERSTANDING HELPS PROBLEM-SOLVING

## Real Problem-Solving

### Jumping on an Untested Solution May Not Prove to Be Fruitful

Imagine you are assigned the task of identifying the causes of a long-standing problem and finding a solution to that problem in your organization. You spend a day gathering some data and find that there is a strong correlation with a most probable cause at hand. Eventually, you assign that most probable cause as the root cause and take some quick actions. What can you expect from this entire episode? Was that really a root cause upon which you acted? Perhaps you might have acted too quickly and those actions could not be cross-checked properly. In this case, you might not obtain the desired results.

In practice, even a small malfunctioning of a machine during a short time frame might trigger a false signal in the analysis of a problem. Take into account the products manufactured during the malfunctioning period. The inferior quality products thus produced require a thorough analysis in order to zero in on the root cause. On first analysis, the inferior products may force us to think ab out the problem associated with product itself, while the actual problem remains with the functioning of the machine. Therefore, we make a blunder when we jump into a solution without first zeroing in on a root cause. Can you relate this example to the various avenues for failure listed previously?

## How to Achieve a Fairly Good Result in Problem-Solving

You may believe that the title of this section should be how to achieve the best results, or perfect results, in problem-solving. However, in this book, we are really interested in following a systematic approach to problem-solving [2]. We are trying to defocus from the aspect of achieving the results. It is presumed that if a structured step-by-step approach is practiced, then achieving results is evident and will be only a function of time.

"If a structured step-by-step problem-solving approach is practiced, achieving results is evident and will be only a function of time."

It is true that problems vary in multiple ways with respect to their depth and diversity. Experience shows that a stand-alone problem may be solved by a stand-alone process. However, when different types of problems come with varying depths and widths, occurring every now and then, it will be next to impossible to discover newer and newer solutions. However, if we approach the problem systematically, the chances of finding the solution are much better.

JUMPING INTO A SOLUTION CAN BE FATAL

Therefore, as the research has shown and as we progress in this book, we will find that a fairly good result in problem-solving may be achieved by following a systematic, structured, step-by-step approach.

### Review Questions

1. Although there are various types of problems, there is a stark similarity among characteristics of the problem-solving journey. Discuss and elaborate on the general and common characteristics.

2. Discuss the three dimensions that govern the problem-solving journey.

3. Critically evaluate how the governing dimensions may impact the problem-solving journey.

4. Discuss and evaluate: Why do you think that when it comes to problem-solving, both a teacher and a lawyer may find a common ground in following a structured problem-solving methodology?

5. Discuss as a team and elaborate on what you think are the reasons for failing to solve problems.

6. Discuss why you think that following a structured methodology is the only way to resolve problems with the least available resources.

7. Critically evaluate the benefits of following a structured method of problem-solving. Encourage your friends to augment and engage in a discussion.

## References

1. Pande, Pete and Holpp, Larry. *What Is Six Sigma?* New York: McGraw-Hill, 2002.
2. Pyzdek, Thomas. *The Six Sigma Handbook.* New York: McGraw-Hill, 2000.

WHEN GOWRIE MET KRISHNA:

*Gowrie:* Now I understand! Problem-solving is a big thing!

*Krishna:* Gowrie, problem-solving is not a big thing. It's a sum total of a million little things!

# 2

## Introduction to Problem-Solving

A problem well stated is a problem half solved.

**John Dewey**

### Objectives

After going through this chapter and understanding the issues described in it, you will be able to deal more efficiently with challenges in problem-solving:

1. *Understand* the concepts of problem, problem-solving, and variation.
2. *Explain* different categories of problems encountered in an industrial setting.
3. *Apply* various problem-solving techniques to resolve issues.
4. *Know* the characteristics of various structured problem-solving methodologies.

### Chapter at a Glance

This chapter introduces the overall general aspects of problems and their solution as observed in an industrial setting. It deals with the definition and various characteristics of nonconformities that result in problems. It also focuses on the properties that govern the very character of a problem and the challenges this poses to a problem-solver.

After you understand the characteristics of problems, we will move on to the challenges one faces while addressing these characteristics. Then we will focus on trying to understand the philosophy and approach of the problem-solver. The problem-solver will remain at the center of this journey. We will discuss and analyze various qualities of problem-solvers in order to achieve the desired results in solving problems.

## The Concept of Nonconformity

Before we start our systematic discussion on problem-solving, we need to understand the word conformity in its actual sense. The word "conformity" signifies "compliance" with standards, rules, or laws. It can be a behavior in accordance with an accepted convention. It can also refer to compliance with practices in vogue. This essentially relates to adherence to some expected set of parameters. In effect, if everything follows an expected and desired path, you should not have any concerns. Extending this understanding further, the word having the opposite meaning from conformity is nonconformity. Nonconformity means that something is not complying with, adhering to, or even following a set of standards.

## Types of Nonconformity

There are various types of nonconformity [1] that may arise from various situations. However, the two predominant types are (a) sporadic nonconformity and (b) chronic nonconformity. A quick comparison of the characteristics of these two types of nonconformity is outlined in Table 2.1.

In contrast to sporadic nonconformity, chronic nonconformity occurs more often. Generally, the reasons for its occurrence are unknown. Since chronic nonconformity is present for some time (i.e., it is chronic), it becomes a kind of situational norm. Therefore, it is seldom acknowledged as nonconformity, and it remains hidden in present knowledge. Since chronic nonconformities exist for a longer time, there are more data for analysis as compared to sporadic nonconformities.

"Chronic nonconformities may offer more detailed data for analysis and improvement."

**TABLE 2.1**

Types of nonconformity—sporadic nonconformity versus chronic nonconformity

| Sporadic Nonconformity | Chronic Nonconformity |
|---|---|
| Occurs occasionally | Always occurs in a particular frequency |
| Experience usually helps in understanding the causes | Usually, causes are unknown |
| Generally accepted as nonconformity | Generally not accepted as nonconformity |
| Quick solutions are prescribed | Immediate solution is not probable but results come from continual improvement |

**CRITICAL THINKING EXERCISE**

Describe a situation that you have witnessed in your professional arena where a sporadic nonconformity in an early stage gave rise to large, unmanageable problems in a later stage. Try to recall that situation and record the steps that could have been taken to stop the emergence of a bigger later problem.

Imagine in a class of 47 students, one student—"Shelly"—enters the class 20 minutes after the normal reporting time. You determine that she does not conform to the existing schedule. This is nonconformity. Her late arrival is also in contrast to the other students' timely reporting to class. You may find that this highlights Shelly's nonconformity.

As another example, imagine that every day Shelly joins the class almost 20 to 30 minutes later than its scheduled starting time. Her late arrival is habitual and chronic. Therefore, you would not generally expect Shelly to be present in the first few minutes of the class. In this case, you would neither mind her tardiness nor search for Shelly in the early part of the class. Hence, you become less concerned about her late arrival. Moreover, since you do not expect her to be present, her absence in the first few minutes does not make any impression on you. After a few days, you become less and less aware of her absence. You may slowly accept her chronic tardiness as normal and fail to recognize the situation as nonconformity. Needless to say that as Shelly's late arrival becomes more of a habit, an immediate solution may not be imminent.

## The Concept of a Problem

On the other hand, a problem is a situation regarding a matter or a situation considered as unwelcome or even harmful; generally, a problem is difficult to resolve. Both nonconformities and problems are unwelcome and undesired. While a "nonconformity" is noncompliance with a set of standards, a "problem" is an unacceptable situation needing to be dealt with and resolved.

"A 'nonconformity' is noncompliance with a set of standards, while a 'problem' is an unacceptable situation needing to be dealt with and resolved."

Considering these two concepts, we may safely assume that if there is non-conformity, there may be a problem, too. At this stage, we need to appreciate the difference between the two concepts. Nonconformity works as a prelude to a problem that requires a resolution.

Further imagine, using the previous example, that you ask Shelly about her chronic tardiness and she tells you that she resides 40 km away from school and takes the first bus available each day. You discuss the matter with Shelly further and infer that in order for Shelly to attend class on time, Shelly needs to relocate closer to the class or using some means of personal transportation. So, the problem at hand is to find a new residence or method of transportation. Therefore, in order to resolve the simple nonconformity of tardiness, Shelly finds herself in the midst of a bigger problem—either relocating her residence or arranging for private transportation.

## The Concept of Problem-Solving

The concept of problem-solving refers to the process of finding a simple and easy solution(s) to complex or difficult issues.

To understand "nonconformity" and "problem" better in the present perspective, let us study the frequency of use of these two words in the last two centuries. In Figure 2.1 and Figure 2.2, we see how many times these two words were mentioned in the public domain from 1800 to 2010. It is clear that the word "conformity" was mentioned more in the first half of the nineteenth century compared to the word "problem." In the twentieth century, and more often in the second half, the word "problem" gains momentum and is mentioned more than "conformity." Because of this, during the latter half of the twentieth century, the words "problem" and "problem-solving" have found much use in the context of quality endeavors that gained worldwide acclaim in every sphere of the industrial and service revolutions.

In this book, we will treat "nonconformity" as a perennial root linked to things or situations that are a problem.

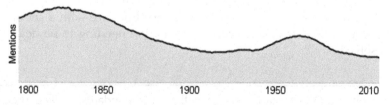

**FIGURE 2.1**
Use of the word the "conformity" over time.

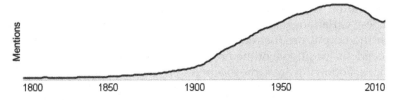

**FIGURE 2.2**
Use of the word the "problem" over time.

## The Concept of Variation

From a generalist's viewpoint, one of the many reasons problems occur is due to variations in the system. Therefore, it is very important to understand the concept of variation as that which causes a disturbance (or disturbances) in a process. Variations may be present in all spheres of life—in the products we produce, in the lifestyle we lead, and in the services we receive or provide.

Unlike "nonconformity," variation deals with deviation from the existing norms [2]. The literal meaning of variation is "a change or slight difference in condition, amount, or level, typically within certain limits."

In this section, variation is explained in the context of an industrially manufactured product. Consider an automotive part that is being manufactured at All Star Auto Products LLC in three successive process steps, such as cutting, drilling, and polishing. For these three processes, there are three work stations installed with three different types of equipment. Three operators operate the equipment. Quality inspectors have observed that the products have variation with respect to diameter of the shaft, radius of the tap hole, smoothness of the cylindrical part, and remnant burrs along the edge of the base plate. In one shift at work, the three operators together produce approximately 345 pieces.

It was determined that there is a considerable variation in these products. On an average, 15% to 16% of all pieces produced are reworked before final acceptance in the assembly line. After critical observation, the different types of variations were listed and characterized. These variations were summarized as to three different aspects—positional, temporal, and cyclical, as outlined in Figure 2.3. Each of these variations has its own way of contributing to the emerging problems.

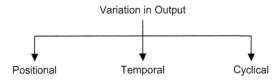

**FIGURE 2.3**
Various aspects of variation in output: Positional, Temporal, and Cyclical.

a. **Positional Variations**

These variations relate to the position of the defects or the properties in the output product domain. These variations occur in different locations (positions) of the product or even the process or work stations. Following are some examples of positional variations:

- Variations that occur due to different machine operators. The operators may be operating the same machine but during different shifts, or they may operate similar machines during the same sift.

- Variations that occur due to different machines. These machines may produce the same product, or they may produce parts of one product.

- Variations that occur in different cavities in multi-cavity molds.

- Variations that occur in different production lines and so on.

b. **Temporal Variations**

These variations occur in a single process while producing a particular product over a longer period of time—such as over days, weeks, or even quarterly. For some process systems, even hourly variations might be very significant. Examples of temporal variations might include:

- Variations in the number of hits on a website over a period of time (hours)

- Variations in mold release temperature during the day and night in injection molding equipment

- Variations in the number of products produced during different shifts in a single day

- Variations in absenteeism of workers measured shift-wise or daily, or for a longer period of time (over a year, etc.)

c. **Cyclical Variations**

These variations occur among repetitive process steps over a comparatively short period of time—typically less than half an hour or even a quarter of an hour. Examples of cyclical variations might include the following:

- Variations among raw material batches made in a continuous weighing bridge

- Variations among input and output aggregates in an assembly line product.

These variations are undesirable and are types of involuntary process output. Also, these variations give rise to potential quality problems in output products. As a result, these variations not only increase the amount of reworking and reject contributions of the entire process, but they also add costs to the

**CRITICAL THINKING EXERCISE**

Besides these three aspects—positional, temporal, and cyclical variations—can you think of any other types of variations?

ongoing production process. In other words, there is a cost associated with achieving the output quality. Therefore, it will be of utmost importance for a professional to understand the nature of these variations, how the variations occur, what are the variation inducing parameters, and to discover ways to circumvent variation.

## Variations Induced by Common Causes and Special Causes

Common and special causes are two very distinct root causes of producing variations in process. Common causes also follow a natural pattern wherein it has elements of a usual, historical and predictably quantifiable variation in the resulting process. In reality common causes are chance dependent as origin of the causes are always available, it may or may not manifest. On the other hand, the special causes are not chance manifestation, but assignable in nature. This means that you can assign a specific root cause to this. These are unusual and unpredictable in nature and not quantifiable while seldom having previous history in recent past. The common cause variations may predictably help us guess the frequency of occurrence, while the special cause variations does not offer any clue for frequency prediction. A few characteristic examples will help us understand these variations better.

Common cause variations are evident through:

a. Some phenomenon always active in any working process: diurnal temperature variations and resulting effects in any process.
b. Predictable variation: sudden increase in humidity in atmosphere after a rainfall.
c. Regular process variations: occurrence of some defects due to skill gap in some operators.
d. A few examples of common causes may be improper operating procedures, poor working condition (insufficient light), measurement errors, uncontrolled vibrations in machines, normal wear and tear, response time of a machine or a process etc. Special cause variations: these are evident through: variations outside any historical experience: development of nausea and other neuro-disorder after sewer gas leak from underground municipal pipe line. There was neither probability not predictability of its occurrence before.

e. Sudden change in process parameters: the cause always comes without any alarm. The variation itself is an alarm. Sudden change of operator in a machine, without sufficient skill training can bring such results.

Special cause variations are evident through improper equipment setting or machine malfunction, poor raw material quality (deviation from standard usual acceptance parameters, absence of the skilled operator in a particular established system, sudden change in operating procedure without due process validation, etc.

The common cause and special cause variations are very important in manufacturing and service quality management in industry since the failures due to special causes can be corrected, whereas failures due to common causes are difficult to correct and these require a sustained effort.

---

## The Concept of Cost of Quality

As discussed in the last section, there is a cost associated with achieving the output quality. Historically, businesses always have assumed that increased quality comes with an increased cost—higher quality meant higher cost. The quality guru, J. M. Juran,[1] emphasized the inverse relationship between the cost of preventing defects and other types of costs. The more money spent on the prevention of defects, the lower the cost of detection of defects will be. He investigated the economics of quality in detail and concluded that benefits outweighed costs.

Another quality guru, Armand V. Feigenbaum,[2] who introduced principle of "total quality control," expanded the concept of cost of quality beyond the manufacturing function. He separated the associated costs into three gross sections: prevention, appraisal, and failure. These cost of quality subsections are detailed in Figure 2.4.

---

"The benefits of investing in preventing failure far outweigh the associated costs."

---

To elaborate further, the following are associated cost guidelines:

- *Cost of prevention* relates to the cost in process planning, monitoring, and training.
- *Cost of appraisal* relates to the cost involved in inspection and testing, audits, and calibration.

---

[1] https://en.wikipedia.org/wiki/Joseph_M._Juran
[2] https://en.wikipedia.org/wiki/Armand_V._Feigenbaum

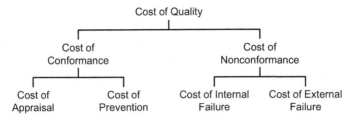

**FIGURE 2.4**
Various costs associated with cost of quality as applicable to industrial context.

- *Cost of internal failures* relates to the cost of rework, downtime, waste, scrap, failure analysis, overtime, and supplier rework/scrap.
- *Cost of external failures* relates to warranty costs, complaint adjustments, goods returned, and costs to customer.

It is evident that these costs are very important and, therefore demand a focus and congruent actions.

> "Generally speaking, so much extra work and rework is performed to correct defects that there effectively is a hidden factory within the factory."

So why should we focus on cost of quality? Primarily, it is to reduce the following:

- **Hidden cost associated** with the process of supplying first-time-right products to customer
- **Hidden loss of opportunity for capacity utilization**, production yields, extension of the market share, and increase in margin of profits

Within this context, we need to focus on solving problems and reducing the probabilities of repeat occurrences of nonconformities (and thus problems) in the first place (see Figure 2.5).

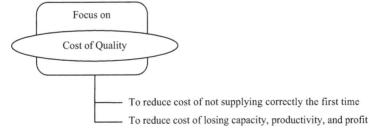

**FIGURE 2.5**
Why to focus on cost of quality.

While dealing with various sets of situations in different industries, we have come across numerous problems. These were sometimes financial in nature, sometimes engineering process-oriented, or sometimes purely personal. While searching for solutions of all of those problems, we came across different methodologies that helped us to find the desired results. In some cases, those methodologies were so helpful that when no solution was available, just following the structured method opened up new roads as options. While we are discussing the omnipresence of problems, the ones that we most often face are those problems we encounter every day in the work place. In the following section, we will see how the problems and solutions unfold.

## Understanding a Problem

Problem as defined by nature have remained with us from time immemorial. There have been problems and, of course, there have been solutions. The effectiveness of a solution can be understood by reviewing several indicators. These indicators include, inter alia,

  a. How, at first, was the problem resolved?
  b. Did all the stakeholders benefit?
  c. What was the cost incurred during the problem period?
  d. What was learned from this difficult experience?

In the last two centuries, after the rapid industrialization in the western world, the focus on these indicators has increased manyfold. Slowly, over a period of time, different professions acquired their subject matter experts, who, in turn, enriched their field of interest. More appropriate strategies came out of specific fields of work. And practicing professionals adapted to new situations with equally newer perspectives.

"We cannot solve our problems with the same thinking we used when we created them."

*Albert Einstein*

### CRITICAL THINKING EXERCISE

The effectiveness of a solution can be understood by reviewing quite a few indicators. Enumerate a few more indicators other than the four referred here that you think are also effective.

In the present time, the world of technology changes very fast. And so it is true for the professionals as well, who change their trade and the organizations they work for, and also for the responsibilities they discharge for their assigned duties. After college and while doing their jobs, graduates encounter newer problems. Sometimes, the same type of problems manifest in different ways. The same problem may require a different treatment in order to reach its root cause.

For example, consider the case of a doctor treating a patient with a neurological disorder or a pediatrician treating a deaf child. Both are trying to solve a specific problem however dissimilar those problems may be. Furthermore, consider that you agree to coach a hundred-year-old soccer club that is under threat of bankruptcy and possible extinction. Or, consider that you are taking charge of an industrial manufacturing unit that has been losing money and has been referred to the Board of Industrial Finance and Restructuring. All these situations pose different problems. What would be your approach for solving these problems? At this juncture, further assume that you are a professional outside the core field of operation of the problem condition. What would you do?

As is seen in the preceding discussion, one specific solution may not work for all situations. We need to devise a general problem-solving strategy that will follow a systematic methodology for addressing different types of problems.

---

"We need to devise a general problem-solving strategy that will follow a systematic methodology for addressing different types of problems."

---

In effect, we are talking about a strategy or a set of process steps that do not allow us to forget the milestones we must achieve or reach for the end results. In this regard, it would be worthwhile to understand the different categories of problems we encounter in our daily work.

---

## Different Categories of Problems

If we try to categorize the often-encountered problems in a professional/ industrial setup, we find that there may be three types with reference to their complexity, span, and nature (see Figure 2.6). They are as follows:

- **Category A:** Just Do It type, which can be solved by kaizen[3] efforts (based on continuous improvement in the operational process).

---

[3] Kaizen (改善) is the Japanese word for "improvement." In business and industrial applications, kaizen refers to activities that continuously improve all functions and involve all employees from the CEO on down to the assembly line workers.

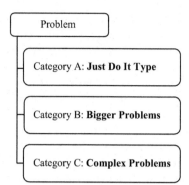

**FIGURE 2.6**
Different categories of problems.

- **Category B:** Bigger Problems, which can be solved by the quality circle (a team of operators), where a strong, fundamental, and functional knowledge is required.
- **Category C:** Complex Problems, which can be solved by a cross-functional team of shop floor leaders. However, irrespective of the categories, it may be perceived that various problems require similar types of treatment. These problems may not be resolved by anyone individually. However, all members of a diverse team will be able to resolve issues together.

## Problem-Solving Over the Years: Modern Problem-Solving Versus Traditional Problem-Solving

Problems have remained with us since time immemorial. However, the complexities may have changed a lot over time. Before we start discussing problem-solving, it would be great to have some ideas about comparing problem-solving methods over the last centuries. The summary listed in the Table 2.2 provides such an overview.

It has been observed that the modern problem-solving approach places more emphasis on process-based thinking and output-oriented group activity as compared to the traditional problem-solving approach. The modern approach also places more emphasis on a multiple skill set than on an individual knowledge base.

"A modern problem-solving approach places more emphasis on process-based thinking and output-oriented group activity."

**TABLE 2.2**

A quick look at the aspects of traditional problem-solving vis-a-vis structured problem-solving

| Traditional Problem-Solving | Structured Problem-Solving |
|---|---|
| Based more on an individual | More group or team-based thinking |
| Individual's memory is tested | Group or team's competence is tested |
| Input-oriented | Process-based and output-oriented |
| Emphasis is on knowledge | Emphasis is on skill set |
| Singular in-depth skill is preferred | Multiple skill set is preferred |

WHO CAN BENEFIT FROM A STRUCTURED PROBLEM-SOLVING

## Different Problem-Solving Methodologies

There are various techniques adopted by different schools of thoughts for solving problems in an industrial, manufacturing, or service sector. There is also a great deal of overlap among all the different methodologies. Each one might be particularly suitable for a specific problem. In the following sections, we will discuss a few of the very well-known problem-solving methodologies. However, the fundamental steps in all these methodologies are equivalent, and they essentially remain the same.

## PDCA Methodology

PDCA [3] stands for "Plan, Do, Check, and Act." This methodology is a generic sequence of work that may be employed to resolve any nonconformity in any sphere of work. These four segments—Plan, Do, Check, and Act—are iterative steps and part of a continuous and endless cycle wherein after the first iteration is complete, the same process steps of Plan, Do, Check, and Act continue in a repeating mode. Therefore, this is called a PDCA cycle. This repetitive cycle gives rise to a perpetual mode for problem-solving and, therefore, continual improvement. PDCA is also called the Deming cycle or Deming wheel and is named after the renowned management consultant Dr. William Deming[4] who improved upon the original idea first developed by Walter Shewhart.[5]

### *Steps in the PDCA Cycle for Problem-Solving*

Though the PDCA cycle's primary goal is for continuous improvement, every aspect of this cycle (i.e., Plan, Do, Check, and Act) consists of various segments of a problem-solving journey. In Figure 2.7, you will find these segments elaborated further for better understanding.

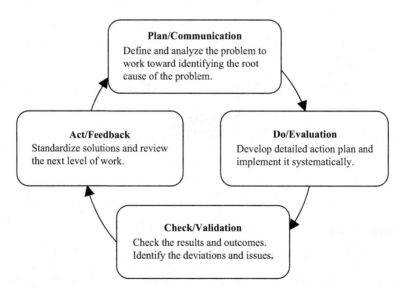

**FIGURE 2.7**
The classic Plan-Do-Check-Act cycle.

---

[4] https://en.wikipedia.org/wiki/W._Edwards_Deming
[5] https://en.wikipedia.org/wiki/Walter_A._Shewhart

The "Plan" part consists of definition and analysis of the problem to work toward identifying the root cause of the problem. The "Do" part deals with developing a detailed action plan and implementing the solution. The "Check" part deals with checking and monitoring the outcome resulting from the actions taken. This also identifies the gap remaining between the desired and the actual state to help augment further actions. The "Act" part focuses on standardizing the various solutions so that a sustainable solution may be achieved.

## DMAIC Methodology

DMAIC (pronounced "də-MAY-ick") is another very popular and well-studied model. DMAIC methodology [4] is at the heart of the Six Sigma approach, which is a long-term, forward-thinking, enterprise-wide improvement initiative designed primarily to change the way organizations conduct business. This approach focuses on a systematic and methodical improvement throughout all business processes. DMAIC, which is a data-driven overall business improvement methodology, is the abbreviation for five different steps—Define, Measure, Analyze, Improve, and Control.

A problem-solver may well ask, why DMAIC? What is the advantage of this process? The five steps in DMAIC set the inherent benefits into action and that action, in turn, manifests in various ways. Next, we will list and elaborate on all the process steps of this model for better understanding.

### Steps in the DMAIC Process

For those unfamiliar with DMAIC methodology, Table 2.3 displays the 12 inbuilt steps of this process outlining the steps' descriptions and quality deliverables.

## A3 Problem-Solving

An A3 report is a one-page document that derives its name from the ISO 216[6] European standard of paper sizes (A3) that measures 297 mm by 420 mm and roughly corresponds to the American tabloid paper size 11 inches by 17 inches, which is laterally double that of A4 paper in portrait orientation. This A3 methodology [5] was first popularized by the Toyota Motor Corporation. They used this concept for writing and developing an A3 report for complex and large data to condense into a concise, easily understandable, logically structured document. An A3 report template is objective oriented and essentially data based. At Toyota, these templates were used mainly for three different types of reports: (a) investment or project proposals, (b) project status reports, and (c) problem-solving.

---

[6] **ISO 216** specifies *international standard* (ISO) *paper sizes* used in most countries in the world today. https://en.wikipedia.org/wiki/ISO_216

**TABLE 2.3**

The fundamental 12-step DMAIC process

| Steps | Description | SSQC Deliverables |
|---|---|---|
| **Define** | | |
| **A** | Identify project CTQs | Project CTQs |
| **B** | Define team & its charter | Team charter |
| **C** | Define the process map | High-level process map |
| **Measure** | | |
| 1 | Select CTQ parameters | Project parameters |
| 2 | Define performance standards | Project performance standards |
| 3 | Measurement System Analysis | Data collection plan |
| **Analyze** | | |
| 4 | Analyze process capability | Project process capability |
| 5 | Set performance objectives | Improvement goal |
| 6 | Identify sources of variation | Prioritize input parameters |
| **Improve** | | |
| 7 | Identify potential causes | List of vital few |
| 8 | Identify their interrelationships | Proposed solutions |
| 9 | Establish practical tolerance | Pilot solutions |
| **Control** | | |
| 10 | Define & validate measurement | Measurement system analysis |
| 11 | Determine process capability | Process capability |
| 12 | Implement process control | Solution documentation |

*Note:* CTQ = Critical to Quality; SSQC = Six Sigma Quality Control; MSA = Measurement System Analysis

Other than the purposes mentioned here, these reports are also used to teach problem-solving in an atmosphere of continuous improvement through the PDCA loop and to create an efficient and shared working environment. A3 methodology works as a powerful tool for all members of the team, including senior managers and even project sponsors and mentors, to imbibe the culture of analyzing root causes and implementing action plans. This methodology also helps all of an organization's stakeholders to put down their thoughts in a concise way and to help each other learn from the resulting story.

### Steps in A3 Problem-Solving

In Table 2.4, we enlist the various steps involved in a manufacturing industry. In addition, you will also find a brief description of the steps and the deliverables that follow after each step. We will discuss these process steps in more detail in subsequent chapters of this book.

**TABLE 2.4**

A3 problem-solving steps

| Serial No. | Steps | Description | Deliverables |
|---|---|---|---|
| 1 | Clarify the problem | Capture the voice of the customer, definition, GEMBA,[7] photos | List of problems/issues, problem definition, observation at the actual problem site, actual site photos |
| 2 | Breakdown the problem | Process map, SIPOC,[8] parts of problem | Process flow chart, SIPOC diagram, bar/line charts |
| 3 | Set the target | To do (what-) from (current state-) to (desired state-) by (when date-). | A target statement that includes the ultimate goal with the time line for project completion. |
| 4 | Analyze the root cause | Interview with stakeholders, use of QC tools | Pareto charts, stratification, 5–why analysis, fish bone diagram, FMEA,[9] etc. |
| 5 | Develop countermeasures | Prioritize issues, identify an effective countermeasure, list possible potential countermeasures; identify and keep tools and equipment ready for change | Brainstorming, priority list, Gantt chart, pilot timetable |
| 6 | Implement countermeasures | Select practical and effective countermeasures; create a detailed and exclusive action plan; implement ASAP | Gantt chart, timetable, visuals, Poka-Yoke,[10] FMEA |
| 7 | Monitor results & process | Monitor progress and report findings Conduct post-implementation review | Run chart, control chart, process capability analysis |
| 8 | Standardize & share success | Document the new SOP,[11] share through horizontal deployment | Train personnel in the new way of doing things, control charts, financial gain analysis, recognize and reward the team |

---

[7] GEMBA is a Japanese word which means the actual working site.

[8] SIPOC is the input-output cycle consisting of Supplier-Input-Process-Output-Customer.

[9] FMEA = failure mode effect analysis.

[10] Poka-Yoke in Japanese means error proofing. To err is human. Errors are inevitable in any process. So are the root causes for every error. The idea is to implement a system to detect the potential error for correction before it occurs. Poka-Yoke is a system to prevent mistakes from happening or to immediately catch any mistake that has happened so that it can be corrected. You will get more detail in Chapter 8.

[11] SOP = standard operating procedure.

**TABLE 2.5**

The steps in 8D problem-solving methodology

| Steps | Description | Deliverables |
|---|---|---|
| 1 | Form a team & list its members | List of team members |
| 2 | Establish problem description | List of issues observed |
| 3 | Interim containment | Process for rejection, rework of product |
| 4 | Root cause analysis | Analysis of root cause |
| 5 | Permanent corrective action | Actions to remove nonconformity |
| 6 | Action and result verification | Verification report |
| 7 | Prevention | How will issue be avoided in the future? |
| 8 | Closure | Closure statement (validation) |

## 8D Methodology

Another technique, known as 8D methodology [6], is used for systematic problem-solving and documentation of the corrective action taken for a non-conformity resulting in unacceptable problems.

### Steps in 8D Problem-Solving

There are eight well-defined steps that help a professional to compose an entire document for a solution. These steps are briefly described in Table 2.5.

For an overview of the aforementioned three methodologies, you might compare the various steps in order to understand them better. We will also try to analyze the interdependence of various approaches and their relationship with one another. In Table 2.6, you will find a

**TABLE 2.6**

A brief comparison of the steps involved in PDCA, DMAIC, A3, and 8D methodologies

| PDCA | DMAIC | A3 | 8D |
|---|---|---|---|
| Plan | Define | Clarify the problem | 1. Form a team and list its members |
| | Measure | Breakdown the problem | 2. Establish problem description |
| | | Set the target | 3. Interim containment |
| | Analyze | Analyze the root cause | 4. Root cause analysis |
| Do | Improve | Develop countermeasures | 5. Permanent corrective action |
| Check | Control | Implement countermeasures | 6. Action and result verification |
| Act | | Monitor results & process | 7. Prevention to avoid recurrence |
| | | Standardize & share success | 8. Closure |

brief comparison. All the process steps are aligned with similar and equivalent steps of the other methodologies. PDCA steps are considered primary steps. Therefore, the process steps of the other methodologies are detailed with respect to the PDCA steps listed in the far left column of the table.

### Review Questions

1. Discuss and give examples for the concept of nonconformity. Distinguish sporadic nonconformity from chronic nonconformity and cite examples.
2. Discuss the term "problem." Explain how problems are different from nonconformities.
3. Discuss the concept of variation. Elaborate how variations can lead to problems. Give everyday examples of kinds of variations and explain their impact on resulting problems.
4. Discuss the term "cost of quality." Explain why we must focus on cost of quality.
5. Discuss problems with reference to their complexity. What are the basic approaches required for resolving these problems?
6. Discuss the necessity and sufficiency of the steps for problem-solving.
7. Discuss and enumerate the main differences in traditional and modern approaches to problem-solving.
8. Critically evaluate how a modern problem-solving approach differs from a traditional problem-solving approach.
9. Discuss use of the PDCA cycle for driving improvements in an organization.
10. Discuss and explain the 12-step DMAIC process for organization-wide improvement.
11. Discuss and explain the A3 methodology for problem-solving and documentation.
12. Discuss and explain the 8D methodology for problem-solving and documentation
13. Discuss and compare the various steps in PDCA, DMAIC, A3, and 8D methodologies.
14. Enumerate a few reasons why people fail to solve problems. How do you think these generic issues may be resolved?
15. How can one achieve a fairly good result using problem-solving methodologies?

## References

1. Gygi, Craig, DeCarlo, Neil, and Williams, Bruce. *Six Sigma for Dummies.* Hoboken, NJ: Wiley, 2002.
2. Arthur, Jay. *Lean Six Sigma Demystified.* New York: McGraw Hill Professional, 2008.
3. Tague, Nancy R., "Plan–Do–Study–Act cycle." *The Quality Toolbox* (2nd ed.). Milwaukee: ASQ Quality Press, 2005.
4. Pyzdek, Thomas and Keller, Paul. *Six Sigma Handbook: An Agile Unified Methodology.* New York, McGraw-Hill, 2015.
5. Sobek, Durward K. and Smalley, Art. *Understanding A3 Thinking: A Critical Component of Toyota's PDCA Management System.* Boca Raton, FL: CRC Press/ Productivity Press, 2008.
6. Rambaud, Laurie. *8D Structured Problem-Solving: A Guide to Creating High Quality 8D Reports*, Breckenridge, CO: PHRED Solutions, 2011.

WHEN GOWRIE MET KRISHNA:

*Krishna:* You lived with this problem for so many years!

*Gowrie:* That's true. I couldn't do otherwise. I have to think out of box! Rather I have to come out of the box and change my perspective to see the problem itself!

*Krishna:* Yeah! It's better late than never.

# 3

## General Philosophy of Problem-Solving

There are no big problems; there are just a lot of little problems.

**Albert Einstein**

GETTING RESULTS

### Objectives

After going through this chapter and understanding the issues described in it, you will be able to deal more efficiently with the challenges in problem-solving:

1. *Develop* an understanding how a problem manifests in daily life.
2. *Know* the general philosophy of problem-solving.
3. *Apply* the fundamental approaches to reduce variation that ignites the creation of problems.

4. *Manage* the common mistakes in problem-solving.

5. *Identify* the competencies, knowledge, skills, and qualities of a problem-solver.

## Chapter at a Glance

In the previous chapters, we discussed the various aspects of problems and their origin. We also introduced a few well-known problem-solving method-ologies. In this chapter, you will learn about the characteristics of a problem and the philosophy of problem-solving. We will also discuss the charac-teristics of a problem-solver—the skills and competencies that are vital for success in problem-solving.

LET'S DISCUSS

## Characteristics of a Problem

From the perspective of a problem-solver, the characteristics of a problem may vary. Among many such characteristics, it is important to ascertain

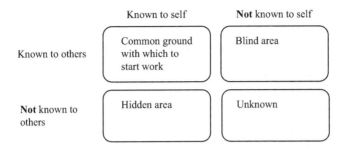

|  | Known to self | **Not** known to self |
|---|---|---|
| Known to others | Common ground with which to start work | Blind area |
| **Not** known to others | Hidden area | Unknown |

**FIGURE 3.1**
The matrix of problem information—known to self and known to others.

whether the problem is known to all concerned. A typical Johari window[1] will help us understand this better. In Figure 3.1, we find a few facets of problem—whether it is known to the problem-solver and whether it is known to others—and their interrelationship.

From this simple knowledge matrix, we understand that if a problem is known to the problem-solver and as well as to others, it becomes a common ground on which to start working for a fruitful solution. Following a similar line of thought, if a problem is unknown to both the problem-solver and others, then it remains unknown. In the latter case, the general objective would be to bring the problem from *unknown* to *known to all.* A problem-solver's ultimate goal would be to bring the unknown situation to light in order to reach a common ground by making all parties knowledgeable about the issue.

## Guidelines for Attempting Problem-Solving

Once we understand that structured problem-solving techniques are of the utmost interest, we must also follow some principles that outline the important facts and guidelines for a problem-solver. There is a proverb that says that a "problem well defined" is a "problem half solved." In essence, it claims that 50% of the solution lies in the definition of the problem itself.

"A problem well defined is a problem half solved."

---

[1] The Johari window is a visual description technique that helps people better understand their relationship with themselves and others. It was created by psychologists Joseph Luft (1916–2014) and Harrington Ingham (1916–1995) in 1955, and it is used primarily in self-help groups and corporate settings as a heuristic exercise, wherein it enables a person to discover or learn something for themselves.

Therefore, it would be of great importance to define the problem thoroughly. After problems are defined properly, there are a few precautionary guidelines for attempting to solve problems. These are as follows:

a. The most fundamental goal of the entire problem-solving technique is to *break the (big) problem into pieces and create multiple small problems.* Obviously, smaller problems are relatively simpler and, therefore, easier to solve.

b. While working toward solving a problem, *one should never initiate any action before creating a hypothesis.* Before creating a hypothesis, one must understand the problem. The "present solution" refers to an action that may remove the present nonconformity that causes the so-called problem to appear. At this stage, we need to understand the underlying theory that causes the problem to appear. We create a hypothesis to this effect. This hypothesis is a logical culmination of a tentative theory. In the following chapters, we will learn more about creating and testing hypotheses.

c. While there may be several parallel ideas that might be effective, *one should never undertake two actions together.* These may affect the problem situation directly. Even these may interact with each other. This is a must, even if we think that the potential causes and the expected outcomes are mutually exclusive, and it will be easier to differentiate the same even if it is thought that the outcomes of all the actions are controllable. The idea is that when we test a hypothesis, the result of the test—the outcome—is not known. This is a decision-making junction and, as a result of this, we want to know whether a test result is appearing in a particular fashion or not. If the test results match with an earlier prediction, then there is a positive correlation with the hypothesis created earlier. Otherwise, there is no correlation. If the test results interact with one another, it would be difficult to arrive at any conclusion.

d. Whenever any action is taken, *allow sufficient time and opportunity for the impact to be felt through collected data,* so that the results are more trustworthy and repeatable.

## CRITICAL THINKING EXERCISE

Try to recall a problem that you might have experienced recently. Irrespective of whether you resolved the problem or not, think about revisiting the old problem again and try to break the problem into multiple small problems. Then, take another look and try to solve the problem again using a different perspective.

## A Few Fundamental Approaches

As we have witnessed in the previous chapter, the ultimate objective of problem-solving is to identify the variation-inducing parameters (VIPs). Fundamentally, there are two basic approaches to determine what key inputs are causing the nonconformities. These are (a) to undertake a forward study of the effects of various inputs and (b) to search for changes or any differences that might have occurred in the system.

There are also a few fundamental approaches used to reduce the results from these VIPs. These are, inter alia, (a) reducing the variation of the measured parameters themselves, (b) converting and modifying the process or product in such a way that its sensitivity to the variation reduces and (c) changing the very way the inputs are made to react in the pre-defined changed process toward producing, so that the problem becomes irrelevant. A few examples will help illustrate the concept further.

### Real Problem-Solving

#### Reducing the Variation of the Measured Parameters—Paula's Fever Teaches a Lesson

Teenaged Paula is suffering from a fever. Her body temperature is about 104°F. We already know that while the fever is a symptom, the root cause of this higher body temperature lies somewhere else. While the ultimate objective is to find out the root cause of the fever and treat it, the immediate step is to find a temporary solution—as a part of the present solution—to provide comfort for the patient.

So, to provide a temporary solution, a doctor may prescribe an antipyretic or fever reducing medicine and, in addition, in some cases, an analgesic, a pain relieving medicine. When prescribing the analgesic, the doctor will advise the frequency with which the medicine should be taken. In Paula's case, the antipyretic may only effectively reduce her body temperature by only 2°F. If the fever at 102°F is still uncomfortable, the doctor may advise Paula to take a full-body bath for as long as 10 minutes in lukewarm water to reduce the body temperature from 104°F to 100°F or more and then to take the medicine. Paula may feel even better if she takes another dose of the medicine, which eventually will reduce her body temperature to about 98°F—a temperature at which she will be comfortable. If the effect of the medicine is reduced after a lapse of time, the doctor may also request that Paula take her temperature at regular intervals to ascertain the correct dose of the medicine. However, the real cause of Paula's fever is still unexplained even though she is comfortable. Here, we are reducing the variation of the measured parameter (i.e., body temperature), while also expending effort to identify the root cause.

In this kind of solution, variations in the measured parameters are minimized and brought to normal. As a parallel activity, the process of identifying the root cause must continue through further tests and procedures, and remedial actions must be undertaken.

## Real Problem-Solving

### Converting the Process or Product into One That Is Nonsensitive—Hard Porcelain Doesn't Break

Let us take an example of a fine-dining ceramic plate manufacturing process. During a particular manufacturing process it was observer that there was high breakage resulting in rejection of pieces during various stages of in-process handling. With the aim of reducing the rejection rate, during the problem-solving exercise, the team made various analyses to understand the reason for this high rate of breakage.

They observed that the green strength (the post-formation flexural strength,[2] expressed in N/mm2, when the in-process product contains 18% to 20% moisture) and the dry strength (flexural strength after the pieces are dried in industrial ovens to contain less than 1% moisture) of the product are less than they should be in ideal cases.

On further analysis, it was found that among various possible reasons, the most important contributors are the inherent low strength of the mineral clay-based triaxial porcelain composition and the low thickness of the rim.

---

[2] Flexural strength, also known as modulus of rupture (MOR) or transverse rupture strength, is a material property defined as the stress developed in a material just before it yields in a flexure test. In a three-point bending experiment, it is defined by the formula $MOR = 3wl/bd2$; where $w$ is the load in kg; $l$ is the distance of the supports (mm); $b$ is the sample width (mm) at the cross section of the rupture; and $d$ is the minimum thickness (mm) of the sample.

In order to increase the flexural strength of the clay-based composition, one needs to take into account various parameters of all the constituent raw materials, and this activity is presumed to be a very challenging affair. It was also observed that increasing the rim thickness of the dinner plates might also help increase the rim strength and, therefore, result in fewer rejections. This also was a relatively easy and fast solution, although it accounted for slightly more material consumption and, therefore, slightly higher production costs. However, the benefit expected from the improved yield (the expected reduction in breakage) would offset the marginal cost increase because of excess material. Other negative implications might be the increase in stack height, which might increase the packaging height. This might also slightly increase the discomfort in handling. Still, increasing the rim thickness might be a potential solution. In spite of these pros and cons, the problem-solving team decided to go ahead with the proposal of increasing the rim thickness.

This is an example of a *present solution*, where the product will be less sensitive to the rigors of in-process handling. As a result, the breakage of products is reduced, and yields improve. In this instance, the handling process is not changed, the porcelain composition is not changed, but the breakage is reduced drastically.

## Real Problem-Solving

### Changing the Very Way the Inputs Are Made to React in the Pre-Defined Changed Process

In an industrial etching process, radiation controlling rare earth glass substrates of hyperbolic shape and eight inch square size are etched by a sand blasting process. The sand blasting is done on the inner surface to aid in adhering multicolor phosphor coatings due in the next process. Since the requirement for production was less, it was standard industrial practice to do the etching process holding the substrate by one hand manually and sand blasting by holding the gun on the other hand. The sand was of specific grain size distribution and the gun was coupled with compressed air at 6 bar pressure.

However, there were many reject and rework as there were variations in the blasting dot patterns, blast density and blast depth. These variations led to variations in look and the output luminance of the final product. After thorough analysis of the defects, it was understood that during the sand blasting process, the pressure was varying, and all the area of the substrate was not exposed to the blasting process homogenously. Moreover, during the manual blasting process, distance between the gun and the substrate was varying, thus changing the pressure and direction of shot; resulting in variation in engraving pattern in one substrate and equally varying patterns across the substrates.

In order to improve the situation, the process control team devised a simple automation process where the substrate is fixed on a plate that can rotate at a variable speed as well as oscillate at a desired frequency. The gun was fixed at a particular distance from the substrate at a particular angle. One compressed air reservoir bottle was placed before the blasting gun control unit.

This way the depth, pattern, homogeneity, and density of the blasting dots were controlled and improved to the desired level. In reality, the team has changed the very way the inputs such as air pressure, sand, blasting distance and its location interact each other in the pre-defined changed process.

---

"The formulation of a problem is often more essential than its solution, which may be merely a matter of mathematical or experimental skills."

*Albert Einstein*

---

## Life Cycle of a Problem-Solving Journey

From conception to completion, the problem-solving journey passes through various phases resembling facets of living a life. The subject experts differ regarding the numbers of phases a problem-solving journey contains. But, a typical journey consists of four distinct phases—conceptualization, planning, execution, and termination. Each phase has a definite outcome.

Conceptualization ⟶ Planning ⟶ Execution ⟶ Termination

---

## The Unified Approach Toward Systematic Problem-Solving

Though there are various schools of thought regarding a single universal approach to problem-solving, the core of these ideas revolves around a few fundamental concepts that constitute the robust foundation of this unified approach. The steps in a robust problem-solving approach provide a set of benefits that help the system to work better altogether, while at the same time assisting individuals in solving problems. A few such benefits are summarized in the following paragraphs.

a. **Root cause identification:**
   This method forces one to identify potential options, single out the most probable one, verify, and validate the root cause. This reduces the overall efforts for quick implementation.

b. **Measuring the problem and the solution:**
   The systematic steps that lead one to the solution also bind one to measuring the data in every step and do not allow one to be swayed by emotion. The robust nature of the questioning technique employed does not allow one to have assumptions that overtake the logical consequences.

c. **Changing old habits:**
   This strong process also does not allow one to have or retain old-school thinking and make the same mistakes again and again. The solution coming out of a structured problem-solving process is not just a small continuous improvement outcome; it is also for break-through events that result in major changes in process systems.

d. **Reducing the risk:**
   This rigorous systematic problem-solving process supports repeated testing and perfecting of the solution, thereby drastically reducing the risks from the process.

In the remaining chapters of this book, you will develop a better understanding of the model methodologies and their benefits.

The ultimate goal of a structured problem-solving journey is to imbibe a culture wherein all stakeholders are involved. This culture brings about gradual change over a period of time and transforming the problem-solving scenario from "no day" to "someday" to finally "every day." In Figure 3.2, the scheme essentially indicates that the structured problem-solving journey brings "everyone" together "every day" to solve problems "everywhere"!

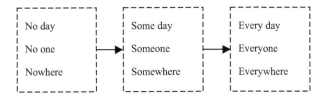

**FIGURE 3.2**
With the help of a structured problem-solving approach, everyone works together every day to solve problems everywhere!

GENERAL PHILOSOPHY OF PROBLEM-SOLVING

## Common Mistakes in Problem-Solving

While one is engaged in solving a problem, there are some easy traps that one falls prey to very often. In such cases, a justified solution is not expected. During the process of problem-solving, one needs to be aware of such flaws [1]. Following are a few such flaws that may significantly change the outcome of the problem-solving process.

    a. Assuming that you know what the problem is without seeing what is actually happening

    b. Assuming that you know how to fix a problem without finding out what is the root cause of that problem

    c. Assuming that you know the root cause of the problem before you confirm it

Please note the word "assuming" appearing in all the points mentioned here. "Assuming" means accepting something as true without asking argumentative questions and getting proof in favor of that truth. Beware of these assumptions because when we make assumptions, we usually close our eyes to a lot of symptoms and fail to receive the signals for a change in direction. And therefore, we become prone to reach the wrong destination.

"While problem-solving, never ever assume, which means accepting something as true without asking argumentative questions and before getting proof in favor of that truth."

## Survivor's Guide

The hero of the entire problem-solving episode is the person in charge of the problem. She needs to go to the problem site (GEMBA) herself. As a leader, she must be at the front. It would be too late if instead of the problem-solver going to the problem site, the problem site were to come to the problem-solver [2]! The problem site is the GEMBA and one has to go to the GEMBA to solve a problem.

KEY ELEMENTS OF GEMBA WALKS

OBSERVE, ENGAGE, AND IMPROVE

GO TO SITE AND SEE

PROBLEM-SOLVER GOES TO THE PROBLEM SITE AND ASKS WHY

USE THE 5-WHY TECHNIQUE

"The problem site is the GEMBA and one has to go to the GEMBA to solve a problem."

There are a few traits that define the success of a problem-solver. These traits revolve around the following aspects where the problem-solver herself takes the charge of the situation.

- GO and SEE it yourself.
- Ask WHY successively, as many times as possible.
- Show RESPECT to the people around you.

These aspects are elaborated further in the following sections. In order to have a perpetual virtuous cycle of a problem-solving culture, as a leader of the entire journey, you have to:

- SET Standards—This is the prime mover. In an industrial setup, the present process may not be standardized. Therefore, changing the present circumstances to align with the set standard is the foremost goal.
- Make STANDARDS VISIBLE—The next task is to ensure that all the local stakeholders know the standards. Therefore, the idea is to make things transparent and visible for easy reference.
- ALLOW everyone to have EXPOSURE to a problem—All the stakeholders are supposed to know the situation so that they understand the problem and the progress in finding a solution.
- Encourage EXPERIMENTATION—This facilitates perpetual learning and gaining valuable experience.
- Accept FAILURE with openness in order to eventually meet STANDARDS—The ability to accept failure is an acid test. This ensures that you acknowledge the failure.

This virtuous cycle of a problem-solving culture takes the teams' experience from the level of ignorance mode to the level of prediction and prevention mode through the rough terrain of denial, accusing, and justification, on through accepting and minimizing, and then to further analyzing and correcting the problem.

In this journey, the leader has to augment a situation wherein she makes the problem visible to everyone, creates a win-win situation where the problem-solving skills of the people around her improve, and she motivates people to move from the stage of outright denial to the stage of prevention before occurrence.

---

"A problem-solver motivates people to move from the stage of outright denial to the stage of prevention before occurrence."

---

## The Problem-Solver's Oath[3]

There are a few insightful mantras[4] that are very important to follow to achieve a sustainable outcome. The problem-solver must be conscious of and trust in these mantras. A few are summarized in the following list.

    a. There can be more than one right opinion based on a fixed set of available data.

    b. There can be one—and only one—root cause for a problem. However, several misguiding symptoms can pop up at various stages in problem-solving. These seemingly prompting leads are usually a manifestation of the same root cause.

    c. The people must rely on data, even if they are not potentially ready to do so.

    d. There can be more than one solution, step, stage, or phase in problem-solving, where all are indirectly and partially heading toward solving a problem.

## The Qualities of a Problem-Solver

It is known to be true that though a team works to solve a problem as a whole, the success also depends largely on the personal character of the problem-solver leader, among many other aspects. The most important characteristics are to be "focused and unassuming." Figure 3.3 provides an overview of the various qualities that the problem-solver must demonstrate in order to solve a problem. Besides being focused and unassuming, she must be able to act professionally and to lead her team members by example. The combination of these qualities will help her achieve results.

## Problem-Solvers' Knowledge and Skill Requirements

If we analyze various skills and the knowledge required for problem-solving, we see that these can be divided into three broad categories. These

---

[3] An oath is a solemn promise, often invoking a divine witness, regarding one's future action or behavior.

[4] A mantra is a word or sound repeated to aid concentration in meditation, a statement or slogan repeated frequently.

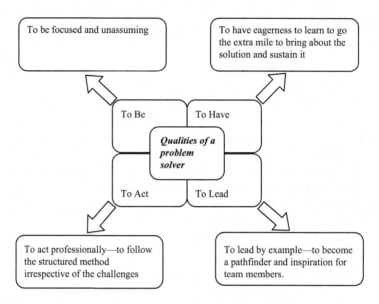

**FIGURE 3.3**
The qualities of a problem solver—the inner qualities of an individual that determine a successful resolution.

are subjects involved, internal aspects, and external aspects. In Figure 3.4, you will find a few pertinent points for each of the categories we mention here.

The list of knowledge and skill requirements is endless. Depending on the gravity of the problem, the subject matter involved, and the aspects surrounding the problem, the characteristics of the problem determine the qualities necessary for a problem-solver. As a problem-solver, in real life, you will experience quite a few challenges that may trigger gaining new knowledge.

## The Competencies of a Problem-Solver

Besides the qualities explained in the foregoing sections, there are a few competencies that a problem-solver must possess to effectively lead the journey

### CRITICAL THINKING EXERCISE

Pause and think again. Review the knowledge and skills requirement of a problem-solver. What further skills and knowledge do you think one must acquire to achieve one's objectives? In addition, you are invited to add pertinent requirements to this primary list.

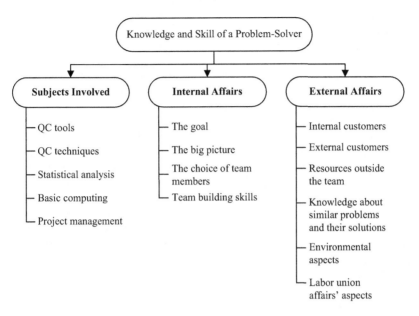

**FIGURE 3.4**
A problem-solver's knowledge and skill ensures that individual's ability to deal with the challenge.

and reach the goal. These competencies pertain to four different aspects: quantitative aptitude, reading, reasoning and critical thinking ability, and writing ability. Some of the competencies paired with these aspects are summarized in Figure 3.5.

Besides having the fundamental abilities of reading, writing, and arithmetic, a problem-solver must be adept in reasoning ability. In every step of problem-solving, one needs to provide logical reasoning to accept or reject various issues that may come up during the course of discussions about a particular problem.

## A Problem-Solver's Experiential Learning

A seasoned problem-solver goes through a structured development cycle in three major areas—doing, knowing, and learning. Figure 3.6 presents these three aspects, which are described in detail in the next paragraph.

### CRITICAL THINKING EXERCISE

How can one begin to sort out the problems that are to be solved?

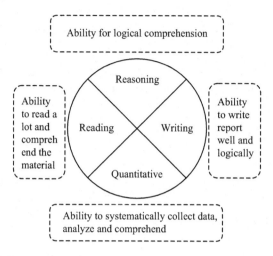

**FIGURE 3.5**
Competencies of a problem-solver.

All our actions take root in the foundation of what we already know. We endeavor to do something using the knowledge we already have. In doing so, we obtain new knowledge. Thus, successive learning is a function of both doing and knowing. From Figure 3.6, learning, L1 (subtending an angle Θ1 to the knowledge axis), results from knowledge, K1, and work done, D2. Similarly learning, L2 (subtending an angle Θ2 to the knowledge axis), results from knowledge, K2, and work done, D1. Learning, L, is connected to knowing and work done in such a way that comparatively smaller knowledge (K1 < K2) coupled with comparatively larger work done (D2 > D1) may well result in relatively larger learning L1 > L2 (angle Θ1

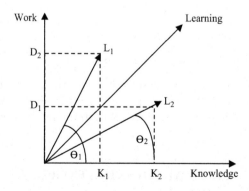

**FIGURE 3.6**
The coordinates for learning as a function of work and knowledge.

being greater than angle Θ2). This empirical relationship between "knowing" and "work done" emphasizes that doing more accelerates the pace of learning.

It is imperative that the problem-solver relies more on "doing" than just "knowing"! In this context, the problem-solver's task is to maximize these areas in their field of operation.

---

"The problem-solver has to rely more on 'doing' than just 'knowing,' for knowledge is of no value unless it is put into disciplined practice."

---

In order to augment a critical thinking perspective in whatever you do, you can ask yourself a few questions similar to those listed here.

- What do I need to know?
- What do I need to do?
- What shall I learn as a result?
- How can I use this knowledge to increase my skills?

### Review Questions

1. While following a few fundamental guidelines for problem-solving, why do you think that breaking a problem into small multiple problems will facilitate problem-solving?
2. Why do you think that one should not initiate any action before creating a hypothesis?
3. What are the fundamental approaches to reduce the effects of VIPs?
4. What are the benefits of structured problem-solving approaches?
5. What are common mistakes in problem-solving? Beside the points raised in the text, can you think of any other common mistakes?
6. Why do you think that showing people respect while solving problems is a necessity?
7. Briefly state the problem-solver's oath. Can you think of any other point that you can add to the oath?
8. Critically think and evaluate how developing problem-solving skills in professionals may help reduce the employability gap in industry.
9. What are the basic qualities a problem-solver should have?
10. Discuss as a team and comment on the problem-solvers' knowledge and skill requirements.
11. Discuss and comment on the competencies of problem-solvers.

## References

1. Pande, Peter S., Neuman, Robert P., and Cavanagh, Roland R. *The Six Sigma Way: How GE, Motorola, and Other Top Companies Are Honing Their Performance,* New Delhi, India: McGraw-Hill Education Publisher, 2009.
2. Pande, Peter, and Holpp Larry. *What Is Six Sigma?* New York: McGraw-Hill, 2002

WHEN GOWRIE MET KRISHNA:

*Krishna:* What is your problem, Gowrie?
*Gowrie:* My problem is that I have no problem!
*Krishna:* Then you must enjoy the sunshine!

# 4

# *Fundamental Steps of Problem-Solving*

The first step in solving a problem is to recognize that it does exist.

**Zig Ziglar**

LANGUAGE OF PROBLEM-SOLVING

## Objectives

After going through this chapter and understanding the issues described in it, you will be able to deal more efficiently with the challenges in problem-solving:

1. *Follow* the universal steps for problem-solving.
2. *Know* the general philosophy of problem-solving.

3. *Apply* the fundamental approaches to reduce variations that ignite the creation of problems.

4. *Manage* the common mistakes in problem-solving.

___

## Chapter at a Glance

In this chapter, we will review the various steps that fill the problem-solver's mind in a problem-solving journey. Using a step-by-step approach, we will discuss all the fundamental process steps and explain their various nuances. The unified approach toward systematic problem-solving requires us to follow a defined path. As you go through these chapters, you will learn how methodical reporting and identification of problems can help you find the root cause of the problem and its subsequent sustainable solutions.

___

## Universal Problem-Solving Sequence

If the entire problem-solving ecosystem is analyzed, it becomes evident that there are four basic stages [1]. They are (a) understanding the symptoms of the problem, (b) identifying the root cause, (c) finding a solution for the present problem, and (d) finding a solution for future sustainability. The last section—finding the solution for the future—also requires one to standardize the whole implementation process. This ensures that the solution becomes a perpetual one and stops the problem from coming back again. A detailed list is provided in Table 4.1, considering all the subgroups that are involved in these four major groups.

**TABLE 4.1**

Detailed segments and steps for a problem-solving journey

| Journey Segments | Journey Steps |
|---|---|
| Problem symptom | Reporting and identifying problem |
| Cause identification | Defining problem, goal setting |
| | Collecting data and analysis |
| | Finding root cause |
| Present solution | Testing hypothesis and identifying probable solutions |
| | Implementing solution and monitoring results |
| Future and perpetual solution | Standardization |
| | Follow-up |

STAGES OF PROBLEM-SOLVING

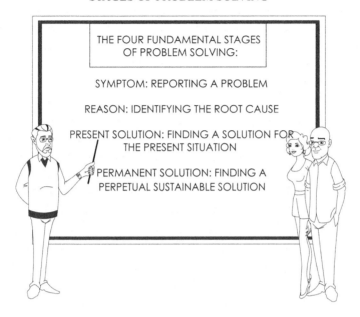

---

## Problem Symptom

### Reporting a Nonconformity and Identifying a Problem

#### *Differentiating a Symptom from a Problem*

This is the first stage of a problem-solution ecosystem. Usually, at this stage, there seldom exists much clarity regarding the problem. The reporter of the problem may be a patient reporting to a doctor, an individual reporting to a chartered accountant, an executive reporting to a project manager, or a wife reporting to a husband or vice versa. The first reporting statement may be as simple and as vague as the problem itself.

Let us use an example. On a sunny afternoon, Simon comes running and reports that there is uproar among the workers. They are agitating on the shop floor. Can you decide whether this is a problem or a symptom of a problem? Actually, you are hearing the front end. Right? Also, the report is superficial. You do not get much information, except a shadowy feel of the scenario. Correct?

---

"In problem-solving, not only the facts and logics are important, but also spatial imagination and vivid images."

Imagine the next scenario. The same Simon comes running and reports that there is an uproar in the polishing section of the shop floor. Approximately, 50 people are gathered there—not only from that department but also from other departments. They have been there for almost 30 minutes. Is this report a little better than the earlier one? Yes, right? This is better reporting. Yet this is not a problem, this is still the symptom!

The first example was full of emotion, and there was no data. This type of reporting uses the language of emotion [1]. In the latter case, a lot of data are available, and that is the language of reporting. It can be easily understood that with the use of data, the language of reporting improves. However, "the problem" still is elusive though a few more "symptoms" have become known. Can you really take an action to disperse the workers or placate them? Nothing is known for which a direct action can be initiated. A problem is that on which a set of direct actions may be initiated to reduce the degree of its contribution. The symptoms only lead us to the actual problem area.

---

"A problem is that on which a set of direct actions may be initiated to reduce the degree of its contribution."

---

Imagine the most popular case of a patient reporting to a doctor about her fever and stating that she is running a high temperature. The doctor must look for the root cause of the fever because fever is only a symptom. Right? The doctor will try to find out the cause of the fever by recommending a few tests and analyzing the results. After analyzing the results, the doctor will have ideas about the possible causes wherein he creates a hypothesis for the occurrence of the problem from the root cause. He then prescribes a set of medicines. Right? He will ask the patient to take the medicines and report back to him about the results/outcomes. If the results show that the situation is improving, then the patient will continue the medicine. Otherwise, the doctor will review the situation and may discontinue the medicine, request a new test, or just change the medicine to a newer, stronger, or a completely different one.

At the very first stage of problem-solving, the focus will be to understand the information and decipher the problem. After we understand how an issue is better reported, we need to learn how to identify a real problem that challenges us to find solution. This stage gives more insight to the problem and some of the issues that may need to be addressed.

---

"The formulation of a problem is often more essential than its solution, which may be merely a matter of mathematical or experimental skills."

*Albert Einstein*

---

FAILURES IN PROBLEM-SOLVING

Here the idea is to get to the point where, in all probability, an action may be initiated. At this stage, it is not very clear whether the identified cause is the only one responsible for the problem. There may be several others involved in producing the so-called "symptoms" that surfaced earlier. The challenge will be to decipher the scramble and find what is causing the problem.

Therefore, when a symptom of a problem is reported, the first and foremost job will be to identify the problem. To generalize, whenever nonconformity is reported, all efforts must be directed to find the root cause before assuming anything or taking any action.

---

"Whenever any nonconformity is reported, all efforts must be directed to find the root cause before assuming anything or taking any action."

---

In this context, let us understand the term *nonconformity*; it would be prudent to take a look at the aspects of a nonconformity. Referring to our earlier discussion, a nonconformity is, inter alia,

- Anything that does not meet a target
- Anything that does not meet the specification
- Anything that does not meet the expectation
- Anything that does not conform to standard

After a symptom or nonconformity is reported, it would be a good idea to run a simple "why-why" analysis to zero in on a workable problem. In Figure 4.1, we find a simple why-why analysis scheme. This essentially details the various levels of reasoning and explains the newer causes at every subsequent step in search of a root cause for problem-solving.

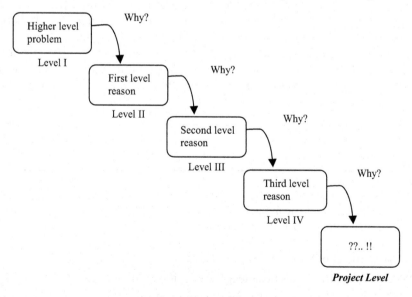

**FIGURE 4.1**
A simple why-why scheme that brings out a real cause.

The idea is to ask a few "whys" successively. This is one of the signature approaches in the Toyota Production System, immortalized by Taiichi Ohno [2]. At a particular step, where we cannot answer the "why", we reach the level where we should start solving a problem. Also in some level of asking "why", we arrive at a point where we may initiate some action. This model of asking successive "why" questions is a good way to understand the scope of the problem. At the last level, where the "why" is answerable, the problem becomes a measurable one, and we can initiate an action that can provide an answer.

"Millions saw the apple's fall. But Newton was perhaps the only one who asked why!!"

You need to ask these questions to understand that a problem is that for which the where and when of the cause is not known with certainty. If the cause is known, it is not a problem. Here we only need to take action. Sometimes, it is attitude or discipline that also leads to the gaps between the desired step and the present step of the problem-solving ecosystem. If the cause is known and suitable actions are not taken, then it is a case of attitude or discipline. In the following chapters, you will learn more about why-why analysis.

IMPORTANCE OF GOAL

## Cause Identification

### Discovering the Root Cause of the Problem

We face many problems in our daily life. If we dig a little further deep into a problem, we come to realize that what was seen in the beginning as a problem, was actually a symptom for a problem.

Imagine a little girl suffering from a fever. She has been running a temperature of 103°F for the last three days. You ask her, "What is your problem?" She replies, "I do not know; I have a high fever." You agree that the fever is not the problem. It is only a symptom. In order to treat her fever, you have to use a structured method to arrive at a probable solution.

You will agree that a problem is actually the absence of a solution. To be more precise, a problem is actually the absence of an idea. Therefore, in solving a problem, we may rephrase this is say that our endeavor is to find the missing idea and that is the solution. At this stage, you start analyzing and doing some tests regarding the situation.

"A problem is actually the absence of an idea. The problem-solving journey is essentially an endeavor to find the missing idea and that is the solution."

On the other hand, a solution is a milestone, which by definition may or may not signal the end of a journey. In fact, a journey is dotted with many milestones. In the continuous-improvement ecosystem of a virtuous cycle, the end of a problem comes with a solution, then a new challenge comes along, and the cycle of improvement continues.

### Defining a Problem and Goal Setting

Once Einstein said, "If I had 20 days to solve a problem, I would take 19 days to define it". The definition of a problem requires one to answer the following questions. (In the English language, these are popularly known as 5W and 2H questions—what, why, where, when, who, how, and how much.) The idea is to ask these questions and find out the answers that will help define the problem. Here are some examples of these questions:

a. *Who* is reporting the problem? *Who* has observed the problem?
b. *What* is reported as a problem? *What* is being defeated?
c. *When* did the problem occur?
d. *Why* is the so-called problem reported? *How* far has it departed from specifications?
e. *Where* is the problem? *Where* is it located?

**TABLE 4.2**

The concept of IS/IS NOT analysis

| ASPECT | IS | IS NOT |
|--------|-----|--------|
| What | | |
| Where | | |
| When | | |
| Who | | |

f. *How much* intensity does the problem have? *How* grave is it?

g. *How* is a problem reported? *How* is it communicated?

## IS/IS NOT Analysis

In this early stage of problem identification and definition, another well-known tool that can be used is IS/IS NOT analysis. This process, popularized by Kepner-Tregoe, challenges one to clarify and agree on what IS and what IS NOT. This may relate to the actual issue involved or what the problem's role is in the scope of the work. The 5W and 2H questions described in the previous section may be extended for an analysis as detailed in Table 4.2. Here, the various aspects of IS and IS NOT are answered through questions of what, where, when, and who. The problem-solver is expected to write down various aspects of a problem in order to ascertain its true nature and to get rid of their assumptions and misconceptions. This exercise brings out the problem from the inside out.

This analysis can be used by an individual or in a group (wherein the team members can prepare this detail beforehand and share the responses among the team members).

Defining and setting goals for problem-solving requires the identification of some parameters of the journey, such as who will lead and be responsible, what one hopes to achieve, and when should that be achieved.

- The milestone—what to achieve as a result of the activity
- The timeline—when to achieve the results
- The traveler—who is to undertake or lead the journey

It is customary to note here that "why," "how," and "where" are not answered in this stage. The answers to "how" will be explored in the sections that follow in the entire journey of problem-solving. The "where" is partly redundant and partly answered by the first "what," the milestone.

"It is so simple. Just ask these questions and get to the core of the problem!"

## Goal Setting

The next big step in the problem-solving journey is goal setting. In order to set goals, the problem-solver in you must ask the following necessary questions to further clarify the situation.

- What problem am I going to solve? The achievement, the goal.
- Why is this important for me to do? The impact.
- How may I do this? The options available.
- Who are my resources, who will help me? The guide.
- Who will be in my team? The coworkers.
- When I should complete this? The timeline for achievement.

After we have asked these necessary questions, we must ask another question to test for sufficiency:

- Will this problem definition lead us to the desired results?

For a realistic goal, both the attainable and time-bound aspects are complimentary. The problem definition and, thereafter, the goal setting should not justify a project end-date that is too far away. Otherwise, it would be too difficult to stay motivated. Furthermore, to obtain the correct input, it is necessary to ask a few pertinent questions to understand the situation better. These are:

- What are the limitations? It is important to know the boundaries.
- Is this possible with the given resources? This ascertains the sufficiency of the resources.
- Is there anybody who has done this before? This is to determine if there is someone with prior experience who can help if needed.
- Are there any real or perceived hurdles that must be tackled to reach the goal in time? This is to understand the other known challenges.

The act of goal setting relies greatly on the interest and the commitment of the problem-solver. There is a great difference between interest and commitment. When you are interested in doing something, you do it only when the circumstances permit you to do so. However, when you are committed, you accept no excuses, only results.

---

"In problem-solving, the commitment of the problem-solver triumphs over mere interest. When you are committed, you expect and accept nothing but results, only results."

---

## Summarizing Informations Through 5W2H Technique

Ms. Viviana works for the Open Stock Bearing Company. A few years back, they faced some problems in assembling lock-nuts in the automatic gear shift assembly unit. The quality control engineers are trying to define the problem with some available data. They run a 5W 2H questioning technique to summarize some available information as detailed in Table 4.3.

**TABLE 4.3**

The summary of the available information with the aid of 5W 2H questions

| Sl No | Questions | Answers | Examples of Input |
|---|---|---|---|
| 1 | Who is complaining? | The internal or the external customer | Ms. Viviana, Open Stock Bearing Company |
| 2 | What is she complaining about? | The characteristics or the nature of the complaint | The lock-nuts for automatic gearshift assembly are out of specification with respect to length. |
| 3 | Why is she complaining? | Problems faced during assembly | The longer nuts are hitting the inner core of the assembly and proper tightening cannot take place, which causes a problem when assembling the gear console. |
| 4 | When is she complaining? | Time of registering the complaint | Date of noticing or registering the problem |
| 5 | Where is she complaining? Where is the complaint registered? | Department/division | Mechanical Assembly Division |
| 6 | How is she complaining? | Channel of communication | Internal report and notes. Discussion during the review meeting. |
| 7 | How much/how great is the problem's intensity? | How many defective parts are there? Have complaints been received from customers? | Defects: 150 ppm, 5 customer complaints received. |

In order we get more information on the character and essence of the symptom and its definition, we are required to go to the Gemba or the actual site where the problem occurred. Japanese quality professionals, during their extensive work with quality and productivity of process systems, have improved upon the traditional system of problem-solving and made significant contributions to powers of observation. The principles that govern these concepts are referred to as *Sangen* principles. These revolve around various concepts, such as *Gen-ba*, *Gen-butsu*, and *Gen-jitsu*. Following are explanations of these terms:

- **Gen-ba**: Japanese detectives call a crime scene the Gemba or Gen-ba. This is the place where a value is created or something is originated. This term essentially means "go to the site or the source." This means going to the site where the problem occurred. When you go to the problem site, you no longer need to make any assumptions. You can see it clearly with your own eyes. Going to the Gemba (the Gemba walk) helps a problem-solver identify, understand, and demystify the problem. It also helps relate the symptom to the actual problem [2]. Going to the Gemba offers a few important aspects to the problem-solver. It offers the feel of a real situation.

---

"A Gemba walk helps a problem-solver identify, understand, and demystify the problem through observing the real issue at the real origin without assuming anything."

---

| The Situation | The Aspect |
| --- | --- |
| Real | People |
| Real | Place |
| Real | Situation |
| Real | Data |
| Real | Solution |
| Real | Implementation |

- **Gen-butsu**: This refers to the "the thing." The equipment, the machine, the conveyor, the work stations, and so on. This is the originator of the problem. During the Gemba walk, a problem-solver has to look for the relevant objects that are directly connected to the problem. These are elements of the problem story.
- **Gen-jitsu**: This terms refers to the facts—the interrelation of the equipment, the human, and other obviously conjoined interfaces. After the things that are connected are identified, the next step would be to understand the relationship among all these elements.

In the defining stage of the problem-solving journey, the Gen-ba, Gen-batsu, and Gen-jitsu steps can aid the problem-solver in obtaining important input.

GEMBA

## Collecting Data and Analysis

In this stage, after the problem is identified, the objectives are set, and the time lines are drawn, further data are collected to get more details about the nonconformity. Different quality control tools are used to ensure that sufficient data are collected and analyzed in a simulated manner to arrive at a conclusion.

### Data Collection

The data, by definition, can be of two types. These are discrete and continuous. The discrete data can only take integer values, while the continuous data may take any value within a range. The discrete data are usually counted, whereas continuous data are measured through a suitable process. For example, the number of passengers boarding an airplane is discrete data, whereas the weight range of a growing baby is continuous data that assumes continuous data as a function of time.

The success of the problem-solving journey will depend a great deal on the collection of qualified and relevant data. It would be very important to develop a well-thought-out written strategy for data collection. During the data collection, there will also be some redundant data that might not be required at all.

---

"The success of the problem-solving journey will depend a great deal on the collection of qualified data and relevant information."

---

So, while planning, the problem-solver has to ensure that the resources are effectively used to gather critical data. In this context, a few general guidelines on the desired process of collecting necessary data are listed in the following paragraphs.

### Guidelines for Collecting Data for Problem-Solving

Collecting data is an art and requires systematic training to achieve certain quality. There are a few guidelines that when followed through in letter and spirit can really help one reach a desired quality.

i. *Remove all assumptions*: As a prerequisite, we need to remove all assumptions from the mind. Assumptions may bring with them preconceived ideas that usually blind the problem-solver who might miss the most obvious things and solutions around.

ii. *Go to GEMBA*: Gemba is a place where the nonconformity originated or the problem is observed. This is the birthplace of the problem.

iii. *Survey the situation and determine the sample*: This is very important as sample size defines the probability of collecting necessary and sufficient data required to understand the problem information.

iv. *Look for changes in the system, process, materials, and so on*: This is very important as it can help identify if there is anything that has changed or deviated from the standard operating procedure that might have contributed to the present problem at hand.

v. *Capture data as they are*: This signifies that one needs to capture data to represent as they happen in the same measuring unit. No special situations are to be created to capture data. As much data should be collected as possible.

vi. *Avoid jumping into a solution*: While collecting data, the problem-solver should not jump into any solution after observing some initial data or getting some initial information that is not representing the whole story. Some data may be misleading, some may be partially directed toward the actual root cause.

At this stage, it is also very important to consider the costs associated with the data collection. Collecting data may well attract additional expenses. In a special case, if the cost of data collection goes beyond the expected problem-solving benefits, a problem-solver has to challenge the thinking process to augment out-of-box thinking to discover or even innovate a newer data collection mechanism. It might also be important to reexamine the situation and look for alternate measureable data. One might also consider reducing the number of samples and sticking to the necessary number of data points only in order to navigate within the available resources.

---

**Real Problem-Solving**

**Scope of Data Collection Affects the Problem Analysis**

Much care must be taken in selecting the scope of the data collection. The following example[1] will illustrate how the scope of the data range selected may make or break a simple analogical decision-making process.

During World War II, many fighter aircraft were hit by bullets from the then newly produced anti-aircraft guns. The authorities directed a group of engineers to design a gun shield for the bottom of the aircraft.

The engineers made an initial investigation of the aircraft hit by gunfire and observed (to their surprise) that the most affected are was the tail portion with 1.93 bullet holes per square foot, which was almost double that of the engine portion with 1.11 bullet holes per square foot. From this set of data, one would surely conclude that the extra shield should be provided to the tail area.

However, among the engineers, Abraham Wald held a different view. He reasoned that the intended protection must be provided to the most vulnerable area of the aircraft, which is the engine area. He further explained that those aircraft hit in the engine area did not come back and actually crashed. The rest of the team understood the logic immediately and found a great loophole in the scope of the sample data considered.

This classic story exemplifies the importance of proper selection of samples for data collection.

---

[1] Adapted from "Abraham Wald and the Missing Bullet Holes" [3].

During data collection, it is possible to have sources of inherent variations. Like in a manufacturing process, the input is transformed into an output product; when inputs to a measurement process are provided, the outputs are observations, measurements and a set of data. During the measurement of some parameters, the inherent process variations may be misunderstood for variation in the measuring system. Therefore, to address the process variability, it would be very important to identify and differentiate measurement system variation from process variation.

### Measurement System Analysis

In order to understand and analyze the measurement system to determine its reliability vis-à-vis its variability, a few terms such as accuracy, repeatability, and reproducibility, all of which are important and necessary, are explained in brief here.

- **Accuracy**: This is defined as the difference in the average measurement between the standard and the observed data. Therefore, less difference means more accuracy.
- **Repeatability**: This refers to the variation that occurs when the same individual repeatedly measures the same unit of parameters with the same measuring equipment. This essentially means that the same measurements may be repeatedly achieved time and time again.
- **Reproducibility**: This refers to the variation that occurs when two or more individuals measure the same unit using the same measuring instrument. This essentially assumes that there is repeatability; the repeatability must be reproducible.

Besides these, we also need to understand two other terms of reference— stability and linearity.

- **Stability**: This refers to the time-dependent variation that occurs when one individual measures the same unit with the same instrument over a long period of time. This focuses on the dependability of the data for the entire period of time.
- **Linearity**: This refers to the consistency of the measurement system and process for the entire range of the measurement. This also delates to the dependability of the data for the entire period of time and measurement.

Variation usually occurs in measurements, and often the measured data set differs from the true value. In this context, two very important terms arise: precision and accuracy. These also need to be understood. The following schematic and graphical representation will elaborate further.

PRECISION AND ACCURACY

Imagine you are using darts to hit a bull's eye. In Figure 4.2, the bull's eye is the circular area at the center of the board. The darts, the filled small circles, are the arrow-hits, which are the measurements. Closely watch the three situations and observe how a classic case is illustrated with three different variants of situation.

In situation A, the darts hit precisely within a very narrow space, but the mean of the hits is far away from the true desired value, which is the bull's eye. Here, they are precise but are not accurate because those did not hit the bull's eye. In situation B, the darts hit the board evenly throughout the board space. The mean of the hits may be considered to be within the bull's eye. The area under the bell curve (adjacent on the right) is greater. Here, the darts are accurate but not precise. However, in situation C, all the darts are within the bull's eye. The hits are within a very narrow space. Here, the darts are both accurate and precise.

During data collection, it is also important to understand the source of variation in the measurement system. The variation may originate from contributions of men, methods, machines, and mother earth.

- **Men:** Skill of the individuals taking the measurement
- **Method:** The process adopted for measuring, including the wrong choice of instrument
- **Machine:** The measuring instrument
- **Mother Earth:** The environment, which includes undesired temperature, humidity, or even vibrations

"During the data collection, it is important to understand the source of variation in the measurement system."

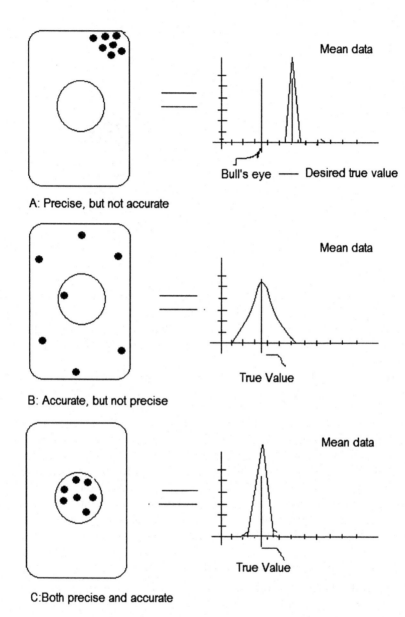

**FIGURE 4.2**
Concept of precision and accuracy.

These are referred to as the four Ms and are identified as the potential sources for measurement system variation.

### Discipline in Data Collection

While collecting data, the problem-solver also needs to be disciplined. A few guidelines are enumerated here.

- *Collect the data from the actual process* and follow the standard procedure. Never adopt a new process of data collection because it might give rise to untrustworthy data.
- *Perform the measurement in the usual environment* using the same gauges as in the process.
- *Collect data through the people associated with the process.* Only they should be employed for as long as possible. This essentially ensures that the variables are reduced to a great extent.

Once the data are collected, it is important to collate and jot down the data in a readable format. Readable formats mean that a large set of data can be reviewed at a glance. This improves data comprehension in the subsequent analysis. This is why format is so important. A beautifully designed and well-knit format may well help a problem-solver do wonders!

## Data Analysis

After the data are collected, the next stage will be to analyze the data. In this stage, the collected data are analyzed to provide some clues by getting to know the trend and the nature of symptom occurrence such as whether the data are uniformly distributed over an entire data range or are occasional or whether the problem is seasonal or spaced over the entire year. In summary, the analysis of the data will provide the character of the problem. The most probable solutions are hidden there.

By analyzing the data, the problem-solver is focused on establishing the various elements of the process, their capabilities, and interrelationships. The idea is to understand the current process in order to take suitable action. Various tools may be used to achieve this objective. Among these are (a) basic statistics, (b) graphical analysis, (c) Pareto analysis, (d) data distribution, and (e) trend analysis.

---

"By analyzing the data, the problem-solver is focused on establishing the various elements of the process, their capabilities and interrelationships."

**TABLE 4.4**

Statistical data analysis objectives and required statistical tools

| Objectives | Required Study | Statistical Tools |
| --- | --- | --- |
| To establish whether the process is reliable | Process stability | Run chart |
| To determine if the process data are normally distributed. | Shape of the data plot | Normality test |
| To reduce the variation and to get the process on target | Spread of the data<br>Centering of the data points | Degree of variance<br>$t$ tests, analysis of variance |

Also, we need to take into account a set of eventual variables that might appear to be important. This information about variables may come from the historical data from the process or even from general wisdom. The problem-solver has to check the dependence of the ongoing problem on these variables. Once these analyses are done, a pattern will slowly emerge. One has to patiently wait till a pattern emerges. It is this pattern that helps the problem-solver find the root cause of the problem.

In this aspect, we must remember the fundamental character of data. A set of data does not have any significance unless and until the data are accurate and organized in a comprehensible manner. Once the data are accurate and are presented systematically, they provide information. Eventually, the information helps in decision-making.

In the analysis phase, the first objective would be to understand the present process that is currently producing a product or service or the problem that needs a solution. This analysis can be done by using statistics. Sometimes logical reasoning may also aid in analysis.

Statistical analysis can be conducted if there are sufficient data either on a full scale or on a sample scale that can represent the entire gamut of data. In Table 4.4, a few necessary studies are enlisted for easy reference.

## Finding the Root Cause

Once Confucious said that men of superior mind busy themselves first in getting to the root cause, and when they have succeeded in this, the right course of action is open to them. When analyzing the problem, a handful of

### CRITICAL THINKING EXERCISE

Imagine that you are working to improve the manufacturing yield of a fast food product. You have taken various steps to achieve the desired results. How can one be certain that the process has improved?
How can one be certain that none of the conditions change or degrade?

information is already available. The next important aspect of the journey is to find the root cause of the problem. The root cause is that which is directly responsible for the problem and on which an action can be initiated. Root cause identification is the most important step in the problem-solving journey. It is a well-appreciated fact that the better the root-cause identification methodology is, the greater is the chance of getting closer to the root cause and the faster a solution will be determined. There are various techniques and tools for a structured search to find a root cause. These can be used interchangeably. Those most commonly used for this purpose are why-why analysis, cause and effect diagrams, failure mode effect analysis, analysis of variance, and so on. The success in this stage will largely define the success in problem-solving.

---

"Success in problem-solving will largely depend on the success in finding the root cause."

---

As seen earlier, a why-why analysis can take you to the real source of a problem, right at the origin. The origin is the place where the problem was born; however, the root cause of the problem may still remain elusive. In order to get to the root cause of the problem, a very simple method is to ask WHY five times and act upon the various stages with suitable countermeasures.

### Real Problem-Solving

**Discovering the Unpredictable Root Cause Through Why-Why Analysis**

GenG Corporation is in the business of producing and delivering GPS-enabled timers for marathon runners. These simple electronic timers help marathon runners get their lap timings recorded and receive short messages on their mobile phones or smart watches. For one such half-marathon event last winter, GenG secured an order for 2,500 timers. The event organizers wanted a special color for the timers as part of a pre-planned branding activity. The delivery schedule was very tight and, in the end, GenG could not supply the timers on time. This caused considerable panic and dissatisfaction in the minds of the event organizers. Let us consider this scenario and see how a simple why-why analysis can help find the root cause of this delay. The successive thought process is detailed in Table 4.5.

From Table 4.5, it can be seen that the successive questions of "why" lead to one answer and then the other. As we go on asking "why," different information comes out in a chain, where all answers are interconnected. Furthermore, as we dig down, a deeper and more fundamental cause emerges. As can be seen in the preceding example, the lead time for the production completion was not considered and the customer

**TABLE 4.5**

Why-Why analysis for delivery delay in supply of marathon bib timers

| Level of Questioning WHY | Delivery of Timers is Delayed |
|---|---|
| *Why is the delivery delayed?* | The full quantity of the products was not ready. |
| *Why are the products not fully ready?* | One of the coloring pigments was not available. |
| *Why was the pigment not available?* | It was not ordered in time. |
| *Why were the pigments not ordered in time?* | The timers were not in the initial production plan. So the pigments were not ordered. |
| *Why were the timers not in the initial production plan?* | The timer order came in very recently. The production plan had been prepared a week before. The minimum lead time for production was 17 days, and customer was not informed about that. |
| *Why was the customer not informed?* | There was other competitor waiting to supply similar products. The order was taken in a hurry. The information was not shared with the team in time. |

was not informed. Had the customer had that information, they might still place the order due to the quality of the product and the persuasion of the sales executive. But a simple lack of communication led to customer dissatisfaction, which is far more costly than the loss of order volume and revenue!!

### Real Problem-Solving

### Why Does the Oil Spread on the Shop-Floor?

Taiichi Ohno, a Japanese industrial engineer, is considered to be the father of the Toyota Production System, which later became the Lean Manufacturing avatar in the United States. He emphasized that true problem-solving requires identification of the root cause rather than the source; the root cause lies hidden beyond the source.

Consider a hypothetical example of five-why analysis that Toyota uses in internal problem-solving training. The problem is oil spreading on the shop floor, which is very common in nature and everyone is very used to seeing this. In Table 4.6, a systematic "why-why" analysis is presented for this problem. Each "why" brings us further upstream

**TABLE 4.6**

WHY investigation questions with the root cause being different from the source of the problem

| Ask WHY | Level of Problem | Corresponding Level of Countermeasure |
|---|---|---|
| Why? | There is a puddle of oil on the shop floor. | Clean up the oil. |
| Why? | Because the machine is leaking oil. | Fix the machine. |
| Why? | Because the gasket has deteriorated. | Replace the gasket. |
| Why? | Because we bought gaskets of inferior material. | Change the gasket specification. |
| Why? | Because we got a good deal (price) on these gaskets. | Change purchasing policies. |
| Why? | Because the purchasing agent gets evaluated on short-term cost savings. | Change the evaluation policy for purchasing agents. |

in the process and deeper into the organization. Beside every "why," countermeasures are given. Note that the proposed countermeasures are completely different depending on how deeply we dig. For example, cleaning up the oil would simply be a temporary measure until more oil leaked out of the barrel. Fixing the machine would be a little longer term, but the gasket would wear out again, leading to more oil on the floor. Changing the specifications for gaskets could solve the problem for those particular gaskets, but there is a deeper root cause that would still go unresolved. You could purchase other parts at a lower cost, based on inferior materials, and because purchasing agents are evaluated based on short-term cost savings. Only by fixing the underlying organizational problem of the reward system for purchasing agents can we prevent a whole range of similar problems from occurring again in the future.

With the completion of this step, the journey segment "identify cause" is complete. After this, one needs to work toward finding the solution for the problem. Finding the solution will be divided into two aspects—the present solution and the perpetual solution. The present solution refers to the solution that stops the present problem; the symptoms will vanish immediately or over a short period of time. After the present problem is addressed, one needs to look at the situation again to ensure that the same problem does not recur. This also requires a systematic approach. In the following sections, these two aspects are explained in detail.

## Present Solution

## Testing a Hypothesis and Identifying the Probable Solutions

### Creating a Hypothesis

A thesis is something that is proven to be true beyond a doubt by using a mathematical or logical approach. However, a hypothesis is something that has not yet been proven. Creating a hypothesis means finding options wherein there are different probable solutions that all seem to be equally likely. Hypotheses may contribute in two different ways. Actions based on hypotheses may either decrease or increase the nonconformity. Either way will provide information as to whether the hypothesis is worth pursuing further or not.

A statistical hypothesis is a statement or a claim about an unrealized true nature of the state of the situation. This is an assertion and a conjecture about some parameters of some population. To determine its truth or falsehood, we need to examine the whole population, which is not practically possible. Instead, we collect a random sample that is assumed to contain all the necessary properties of the entire data population. We use this data to support the claim or the assertion that is the hypothesis. Thus, we draw a conclusion based on statistical significance, which is an inference about the population set determined from the collected sample data.

In this case, it is very important to understand the term *null hypothesis*. A null hypothesis is an assertion about a parameter from the entire set of data that we hold as true unless there is sufficient statistical evidence to deduct and conclude that it is false. The negation of a null hypothesis is called an *alternative hypothesis*. For example, during a process study, one quality assurance officer claims that the average number of customer complaints per month is at most 10. Therefore, the average, $\mu$, is $\leq 10$. Therefore, the null hypothesis is denoted as $H_0 = \mu \leq 10$. The alternative hypothesis will be denoted as $H_1 = \mu > 10$.

The problem-solver's objective would be to create as many hypotheses as possible. The greater the number of hypotheses, the greater the number of probable solutions and, therefore, the more possibilities there are for making a breakthrough.

| Null Hypothesis ($H_0$) | Alternative Hypothesis ($H_1$) |
|---|---|
| This usually describes the status quo—the present state of affairs. | This usually describes the opposite or a difference. |
| This also refers to the first assumption that we accept unless otherwise proven. | |
| This is the hypothesis that we reject or fail to reject based on the evidence gathered. | |

### Testing a Hypothesis

"I have learned more from my mistakes than from my successes."

*Sir Humphrey Davy*

Hypothesis testing is the process of determining whether a given hypothesis is true or not. Usually, hypothesis testing is done through statistical means. To improve a process, we need to identify factors that affect the statistical mean and standard deviation. Once we have identified these factors and taken proper action for betterment, we need to validate actual improvement in the process. Testing a hypothesis by statistical means is also warranted when we cannot decide what the differences are among processes by simple graphical means. By testing a hypothesis using logical reasoning or the application of statistics, everyone makes the same decision.

"By testing hypothesis using logical reasoning or the application of statistics, everyone makes the same decision."

In a general sense, an experiment may be designed to suitably check whether a hypothesis is true or false. In this stage of problem-solving, all the hypotheses are tested one by one to check, verify, and validate the relevance of these to the nonconformity or to that situation the problem-solver is attempting to resolve. Here the work flow proceeds as follows.

- Create multiple hypotheses.
- Check the first hypothesis; conduct some tests.
- If the results are encouraging, continue with the same hypothesis and plan experiments that favor it.
- If the results are not encouraging, then go to the next hypothesis and plan experiments accordingly.

Earlier, we said that a null hypothesis is considered to be true if there is no sufficient evidence against it. If an alternative hypothesis is accepted, then the null hypothesis is false and vice versa.

### Gathering the Data and the Concept of Sampling

After the null and alternative hypotheses are determined, the success of hypothesis testing depends heavily on gathering evidence. Needless to say, the only evidence is data that leave no uncertainty. At this particular stage, we have to be very cautious. If we can check 100% of the data set, then we will have theoretically perfect evidence.

Take the example of a pin-making machine. If we can obtain 100% of the pins coming out of the machine and calculate the population mean, then we have perfect evidence and can easily tell whether the corresponding null hypothesis is true. However, the measuring parameter for 100% of the sample is impossible. Not only is this a ridiculous task, but also not all the pins have been produced yet. Even if they were all produced, the time, effort, and cost involved in collecting such a sample would be too large to be practical. In these kinds of situations, the evidence is gathered from analysis of a random sample population.

---

"In random sample analysis, we cannot be 100% confident."

---

The degree of our confidence will depend on several parameters—size, distribution, and random sampling technique. We need to optimize the random sample size in order to obtain reliable data within the desired time and cost parameters. In practical situations, we may be forced to decide on some null hypothesis with insufficient data. For example, in the manufacturing sector, a quality control engineer has to accept or reject a proposed new material based only on a random sampling procedure, or a human resources manager has to accept or reject candidates on the basis of an interview. You usually will buy a car based on a test drive.

When we make decisions on evidence without 100% confidence, mistakes may occur. There are two types of these mistakes or errors—Type I and Type II. The acceptance criterion for the truth in hypothesis testing is summarized in the matrix diagram in Figure 4.3. Note the two quadrants with the correct decisions. When the null hypothesis is true and we accept the null hypothesis, then we take a correct decision. However, we commit Type I error when we Reject $H_0$ when $H_0$ is true. The probability of committing this error is denoted as $\alpha$. Therefore, $(1 - \alpha)$ is the probability of accepting $H_0$ when $H_0$ is true. Similarly, we commit Type II error when we accept the null hypothesis, when alternate hypothesis is true.

Type I error: Reject $H_0$ when $H_0$ is true.

    $\alpha$: The probability of making a Type I error.

    $1 - \alpha$: The probability of accepting $H_0$ when $H_0$ is true.

Type II error: Accept $H_0$ when $H_a$ is true.

    $\beta$: The probability of making a Type II error.

There is no error when a true null hypothesis is accepted and a false null hypothesis is rejected. We commit a Type I error when we reject a true null hypothesis, and we commit Type II error when we accept a false null hypothesis.

|  |  | Truth | |
|---|---|---|---|
|  |  | $H_0$ | $H_a$ |
| $H_0$<br>Accept | | Correct Decision | Type II |
| $H_a$ | | Type I | Correct Decision |

**FIGURE 4.3**
Decision matrix for hypothesis testing—truth versus acceptance.

"Hypothesis is perhaps the most powerful tool, man has invented to achieve dependable knowledge"

*Fred Kerlinger*

In order avoid Type I and II errors, we must not always try to accept or reject the null hypothesis. This would be foolish as we may not have sufficient information to arrive at the same conclusion. Ideally, we should try to minimize the errors and settle for some optimal probability of each type of error. There are other parameters such as the "credibility rating," *p*-value, and the "significance level," $\alpha$ (pronounced as alpha)—the maximum probability of a Type I error, and $\beta$ (pronounced as beta)—the maximum probability of Type II error, that are very important to complete our understanding of the statistical test of a hypothesis. The component $\beta$ $(1 - \beta)$ is better known as the *power* of the hypothesis test. This power can be defined as the probability that a false null hypothesis will be detected by testing that hypothesis.

### Real Problem-Solving

#### Innocence Till Proven Guilty Beyond a Reasonable Doubt

Under the legal system of the United States and many other countries, an accused individual is assumed to be innocent unless and until proven guilty "beyond a reasonable doubt." As per our discussion, the null hypothesis that the accused is innocent. We will hold that as true until we prove it is false beyond a reasonable doubt. The alternate hypothesis is that the accused is guilty. Figure 4.4 shows a decision matrix concerning the verdict versus the truth.

|  | Truth | |
|---|---|---|
|  | $H_0$ Innocent | $H_a$ Guilty |
| Verdict $H_0$ Set Free | Innocent, Set Free  Correct Decision | Type II |
| $H_a$ Guilty & Sentenced | Type I | Guilty, Sentenced  Correct Decision |

**FIGURE 4.4**
Decision matrix for hypothesis testing—verdict versus truth.

**TABLE 4.7**

Summary of hypothesis testing: continuous Y, discrete X

| Tests | Null Hypothesis Properties | Alternative Hypothesis Properties |
|---|---|---|
| 1. Run chart | $H_0$: There are no trends | $H_a$: There are trends |
| 2. Normality test | $H_0$: Data shows normal distribution | $H_a$: Data does not show normal distribution |
| 3. Homogeneity of variance | $H_0$: $\sigma_1 = \sigma_2$ | $H_a$: $\sigma_1 \neq \sigma_2$ |
| 4. Sample t-test | $H_0$: $\mu = 50$ | $H_a$: $\mu \neq 50$ |
| 5. Sample t-test | $H_0$: $\mu_1 = \mu_2$ | $H_a$: $\mu_1 \neq \mu_2$ |
| 6. Analysis of variance | $H_0$: $\mu_1 = \mu_2 = \mu_3 = \mu_4$ | $H_a$: At least one $\mu$ is different from others |

In the context of gathering data by sampling technique or by conducting experiments to test hypothesis, two typical situations will arise. The independent data variable (denoted as X) can be discrete, whereas the dependent variable data (denoted as Y) can be both continuous and discrete.

Consider the example of a baby's growth over a specific period of childhood years. Her weight (Y) will increase continuously as a function of years of age (X). Here, the dependent variable (Y) is continuous, but the input independent variable (X) in years is discrete. For hypothesis testing, we may use a few statistical tools, such as a run chart, normality test, homogeneity of variance, t-test, and analysis of variance. Table 4.7 presents a summary of all the tests for a quick review.

Consider the example of an automobile engine. Internal combustion engines are characterized by the number of cylinders they have, the volume of the cylinder displacement, and the number of strokes they provide per cycle. For a given number of strokes and the number of cylinders, an automobile engine will produce a power corresponding to the volume of the cylinder displacement. For every input value of discrete displacement data (X), the resulting engine power (Y) will be a discrete value. A summary of all tests for such cases is presented in Table 4.8.

"In problem-solving, not only the facts and logics are important but also the spatial imagination and vivid images."

In Table 4.7, we find a few tests to conduct hypothesis testing such as normality test, homogeneity of variance, sample t-test and analysis of variance. We will not discuss much about the statistical tests here. For a more in-depth understanding of hypothesis testing, the reader may refer to further works on this aspect of statistics. However, for the sake of brevity and keeping our focus on the core subject of problem-solving, we will restrict ourselves up to this point. In the following chapters, these statistical tools will be described more in detail.

**TABLE 4.8**

Summary of hypothesis testing: discrete Y, discrete X

| Tests | Null Hypothesis Properties | Alternative Hypothesis Properties |
|-------|---------------------------|-----------------------------------|
| 1. Run chart | $H_0$: There are no trend | $H_a$: There are trends |
| 2. Normality test | $H_0$: Data shows normal distribution | $H_a$: Data does not show normal distribution |
| 3. Sample t-test | $H_0$: $\mu = 50$ | $H_a$: $\mu \neq 50$ |
| 4. Sample t-test | $H_0$: $\mu_1 = \mu_2$ | $H_a$: $\mu_1 \neq \mu_2$ |
| 5. Analysis of variance | $H_0$: $\mu_1 = \mu_2 = \mu_3 = \mu_4$ | $H_a$: At least one $\mu$ is different from others |
| 6. Scatter plots | Scatter diagrams are a visual tool used to depict the dependency relationship of cause and effect between the input and output. | |

### Identifying a (Probable) Solution

After the hypotheses are tested, it will be obvious that all of the possible solutions are not yielding results. There will be one or two tests indicating that the solution may be within. Those steps should be identified and undertaken for further action. Those tests show a positive correlation with the problem reported.

# Implementing Solutions and Monitoring Results

"You cannot cross the sea merely by standing and staring at the water."

*Rabindranath Tagore*

## Implementing a Solution

At this stage, physical resources are gathered and one should take stock of the situation. The resources are considered and an action plan is laid out for implementation. As a guideline for implementing new problem-solving ideas, it is always preferable to implement the solution in one part of the affected process. This approach will work as a pilot trial before we deploy all the desired actions. Usually at this point, the control points or the parameters are changed according to the earlier test results. Detailed data collection and data analysis is also planned to validate the actions taken.

A trend chart showing the evolution of the results over the period of "before" and "after" the actions are taken will be a good measure for evaluating the merits. An absolute result, a daily trend, or a weekly trend will suffice. The review of results will show whether the implemented actions are producing the desired results. If all the results are not satisfactory, one needs to return to the discussion table to determine why the desired results are not achieved. In special cases, the situation might also call for a reversal of actions and implementation of a completely new solution.

"While implementing solutions, during the pilot trials, plan for detailed data collection and analysis to validate the actions that are implemented."

## Monitoring Results

After the probable preventive or corrective actions are implemented, it is important to monitor the results and the changed processes, if any. We need to identify the parameters to be measured for the performance appraisal of the new process. There are a few key points that need to be remembered for a successful monitoring phase. These are necessary to make certain that the solutions are implemented properly. The points to remember are:

- Where is the location of the data collection?
- What are the data taken for products and processes?
- Is a special instrument or a new measurement method employed?
- When is the data collected?
- Who will review and document the data?

In the monitoring stage, we need to constantly keep an eye on the output results to be certain that the same problem does not surface again.

FOLLOW-UP AND MONITORING

### Planning a Standardized Response in the Case of Failure

After the first solutions are implemented, there still will be a chance that negative feedback will be received about the implemented changes in the process. Therefore, before the changes are made permanent throughout the whole process, we need to ascertain that the proposed changes are implemented on a pilot scale for a few aspects of this stage. The following questions will help understand this better.

- Who takes action post-review and analyzes the data?
- What kind of failure may occur?
- What action should be undertaken in case of a process failure?
- Are maintenance or troubleshooting procedures available? If so, where may these be found? How will the responsible individual be able to access them?

## Perpetual Solution

### Standardizing the New Process or Method

After the present solutions are implemented, the next step would be to find a solution that ensures perpetual avoidance of the problem. This part is as tricky as finding the present solution has been. This requires some experience and skill to ensure that a comprehensive action or a step is taken. This is discussed in more detail in the following section.

In a manufacturing setup, we need to take a step or two backwards in the process to find out what possible action might help the problem-solver to eliminate the reoccurrence of the problem. Some extra controls in the process system might be necessary to ensure that the same nonconformities in the system do not appear again and again. This step requires a careful study to understand the impact of the preceding process steps on the subsequent process steps. This may also require one to take steps to ensure that the support functions of the main process are also performed under controlled guidance.

In this stage, the concept of mistake-proofing will be introduced. This concept can be explained using a Japanese methodology called Poka-Yoke (pronounced as Pokah-Okay), which literally means mistake-proofing. There are a few techniques for understanding Poka-Yoke implementation.

Standardization is the process of making an existing system or a new system conform to a standard. This tool is used to ensure that the improvements made throughout the problem-solving journey are sustained. Unless the problem-solver puts all the details and changes in a proper document, the benefits, in all probability, will be lost in a short time. In actuality, all successful problem-solving journeys end with some gains that need to be maintained when facing more and more challenges. Setting the standards and following them helps us hold onto those gains.

EFFECTIVE MONITORING MUST
HAVE THESE ELEMENTS

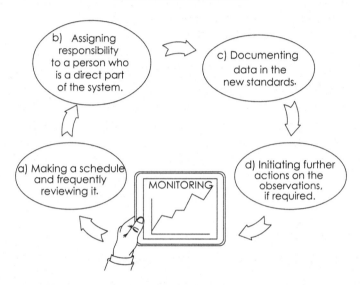

As a part of the standardization process, preparing the standard operating procedure (SOP) in consultation with all the stakeholders will be very crucial. This is also a part of the process–change–management work flow. This activity also allows the downstream processes to proceed smoothly.

At this stage, the problem-solver has to make a few changes in the systems to accommodate the implemented actions as a new method of operation. As per any new requirement, documents need to be created. It is normal to have SOPs in place for any process steps. The SOPs should be scrutinized to see what changes made in the process differ from current procedures. Those changes should then be incorporated in the SOP and published internally, thereby informing all the stakeholders of these changes.

At this stage, we also need to develop and implement a plan to control the new method of operation. Besides training a new set of people to work under controlled guidance, introducing a Poca-Yoke solution, or creating new work instructions and SOPs, there are other steps that can also be taken. As a part of the standardization process, the following actions may also be warranted.

a. Filling out a checklist at the proper times
b. Fixing alarms to indicate the onset of any nonconformity
c. Displaying control charts for better visual control
d. Evaluating the possibilities of horizontal deployment

## Following Up

Follow-up and monitoring means observing and checking the progress of the actions taken during problem-solving for a specified period of time. This is a systematic process of collecting, collating, analyzing, and using data to evaluate the effectiveness of any observation made and any changes brought on as a result of problem-solving.

Similar to the thermodynamic world, a problem-solution journey revolves around the concept of entropy. The law of entropy states that the randomness of the world always tends to increase. This essentially means that after the solutions are determined and some specific actions take place, the new order will try to dilute those action over time if follow-up mechanisms are not put in place. Once the standardization is complete, we need to frequently review and ascertain whether the new standards are put in place and followed properly.

This follow-up and monitoring phase is facilitated by the use of run charts, control charts, and improved process capability analysis. During this phase, it is advisable to allow the process to continue to perform in the usual way without disturbing it with frequent undesirable changes. Unless warranted, we must try not to change any parameters of the ongoing process. In general problem-solving methodology, the investigation or the change in a parameter is warranted if data points in the control chart behave in a particular way. Subsequent chapters of this book will discuss the use of control charts in more detail.

---

"During the monitoring phase, allow the process to perform undisturbed without any changes."

---

At the start of this process, it may be justifiable to monitor the results more often, such as every working shift or every day. However, as time passes, the monitoring frequency may be reduced to weekly once or even less often. This essentially means that once the standards are set, the system should be automated such that monitoring becomes a part of the new process and a special review of the process becomes less and less necessary. The systematic review at the follow-up and monitoring stage must lessen giving rise to more trust in the system and resulting in increased robustness.

Successful follow-up and monitoring enables the result-oriented process change management. Effective monitoring must have the following elements to successfully close the problem-solving episode and achieve its results:

a. Making a schedule and frequency of review
b. Assigning responsibility for monitoring to a person who is a direct part of the system
c. Reviewing and cross-checking against the new SOP and documenting the data in the new standard
d. Initiating further actions on the observations but only if warranted

### Review Questions

1. In the discussion of the general philosophy of problem-solving, which part do you relate to the most and why?

2. While studying the universal problem-solving sequence, evaluate and explain how the different steps complement each other.

3. Discuss as a team how why-why analysis may help one to zero in on the actual problem site.

4. Discuss how 5W-2H questions may help one define the problem.

5. Critically think and evaluate the concepts of milestones and time lines.

6. Explain the concept of goal setting.

7. Explain why hypothesis creation is very crucial in the problem-solving journey.

8. Explain with examples why and how the concept of Poka-Yoke is very important in sustainable problem solutions.

9. Discuss as a team and explain how continual improvement rests upon the foundation of standardization.

### References

1. Sugiura, Tadashi and Yamada, Yoshiaki. *The QC Storyline: A Guide to Solving Problems and Communicating the Results.* Tokyo: Asian Productivity Organization, 1995.
2. Shiba, Shoji and Walden, David. *Breakthrough Management.* New Delhi: Confederation of Indian Industry, 2006.
3. Ellenberg, Jordan. *How Not To Be Wrong: The Power of Mathematical Thinking.* New York: Penguin Books, 2014.

WHEN GOWRIE MET KRISHNA:

*Gowrie:* When do you think that you will be able to solve this problem?
*Krishna:* When you confront a problem, you begin to solve it. Precisely, that's what I am doing now!

# 5

## Techniques and Tools for Generating Ideas and Organizing Basic Information

I have learned more from my mistakes than from my successes.

**Sir Humphrey Davy**

## Objectives

After going through this chapter and understanding the issues described in it, you will be able to deal more efficiently with the challenges in problem-solving:

1. *Formulate* ways to generate fruitful ideas.
2. *Conduct* successful brainstorming and multi-voting sessions.
3. *Avoid* red herrings and not get distracted when capturing ideas and opinions.
4. *Reintegrate* ideas into a workable cause-and-effect diagram that encapsulates all opinions.

## Chapter at a Glance

In this chapter, many facets of quite a few techniques and tools that usually are employed to generate ideas and organize basic information are discussed in detail. However, these techniques and tools are addressed separately in the context of problem-solving; more than one tool may be used when the techniques are employed. The techniques such as brainstorming and multi-voting are generic in nature, and these can be used holistically across different segments of the problem-solving journey. The tools—such as an affinity diagram, tree diagram, SIPOC diagram (an acronym for Supplier, Input, Process, Output, and Customer), process flow chart, and cause and effect diagram—are discussed in more detail in the context of industrial problem-solving. A close look at the examples given will help the reader learn more about the subject matter.

## Techniques for Generating Ideas and Organizing Basic Information

### Brainstorming

Brainstorming is a process of discussion that a joint program of thinking among colleagues and working team members who have a stake in finding a desired result befitting and benefiting all [1]. Brainstorming sessions essentially are dialogues among members, where everybody presents their ideas naturally. This process can help the team reach a common goal. This technique can be used in almost all spheres of life and probably has been used since time immemorial. In prehistoric times, the hunter-gatherers must have come back to their base camp and discussed in detail the imminent dangers they faced or new ideas they had. This was the same as brainstorming!

"When people join together and think in a synergistic manner, a five times greater output is achieved."

To conduct a successful brainstorming session, we need to adhere to a few general guidelines that help our creative thinking process develop into the outline of a fully grown solution. During a brainstorming session, the participating team members have to be focused on finding realistic and specific action points. As a result, a measurable achievement may come within a limited time.

In a brainstorming session, when as many as eight to ten team members are discussing an issue, there is every probability that deviations may occur in thinking and the group may be diverted occasionally. Therefore, the success of a brainstorming session will largely depend on the team members' systematic and disciplined approach toward finding a solution. If these sessions are not focused and not properly administered, the desired results will not be attained.

A successful brainstorming session requires a few fundamental elements. These are outlined in the following section.

## Basic Requirements

1. *The objectives*
   To start with, when brainstorming, we need a specific challenge that is faced by the group. It is best to have an open-ended question that the group is trying to answer.

2. *The team strength*
   Ideally, there may be 8 to 12 people in a brainstorming session. Depending on the gravity of the issue at hand, there may be fewer people in the group. However, having more people in the group does not necessarily imply a better discussion. The point is to encourage a greater number of ideas.

3. *The leader*
   There must be a discussion leader who will guide the team members in a fruitful session.

## Mantras for a Successful Session

Once we understand the basic requirements for a fruitful session, we will focus on aspects of successfully conducting the session. The leader and the group members are expected to know about the problem in advance. They need to follow a few simple mantras for a successful session.

1. *Topic introduction*
   First, the leader introduces the topic or question to the group. She may also make a short presentation about the context in question and its impact on the present scenario. If required, she may provide a few written documents dealing with relevant data. Though this can be done before the discussion starts, the reference to this data is mandatory in

the session. She also will highlight why the issue is important and what the outcome of the brainstorming session means to the group. This will help the group focus on the discussion. The leader also announces a realistic time period in which the members will be allowed to deliberate. Depending on the topic, it may be one to two hours.

2. *Generating ideas*
   After the group understands the problem, the leader may prompt the group to think about it and come up with some ideas. All ideas are welcome. No idea will be criticized.

---

"While generating ideas, all ideas are welcome, no idea will be criticized."

---

The purpose is to come up with as many ideas as possible and not to lose even a single crazy idea. All the group members are motivated not only to think about their ideas but also to advance and follow through with the ideas of others. At the birth of an idea, the notion may seem crazy, but the leader may help the group discuss that particular idea to obtain a matured outcome. No idea should be discarded unless it is totally out of context. Following are a few rules of thumb.

- Defer judging the concepts or ideas; do not allow discussion and evaluation.
- Allow ideas to be built upon and develop the ideas of others.
- Motivate participants to think and allow sufficient time for that to take place.
- Allow only one conversation at a time and avoid cross talking.
- Bring the team into focus if they move away from the core issue.
- Encourage wild ideas because those may bring in new concepts.
- Every idea must be recorded unless it is obviously wrong and not acceptable.

3. *Recording the ideas*
   The leader of the session or someone designated will record the ideas. This recording can be on a writing board in the form of a list or in a mind map, where all members can see the information for a common understanding. Ideas are recorded verbatim, and keywords and short phrases are captured for reference without much discussion because an idea could be nipped in the bud. A listing of all the ideas may also be circulated among the members of the group.

4. *Evaluating ideas*
   Once the first phase of idea generation is complete, an idea evaluation may take place at a subsequent session. This session may be held immediately after the first session or may be held after some

time has passed. The leader considers the listed ideas one by one for further discussion where all the team members deliberate and assign a kind of priority number with respect to importance, relevance, urgency, and so on with respect to the problem. Once the ideas are agreed upon, the team must accept these en masse. Every individual and the group as a whole must take responsibility for this decision.

---

"Once the ideas are agreed upon, the team must accept these en masse. Every individual and the group as a whole must take responsibility for this decision."

---

5. *Outcome of the brainstorming session*
   After all the previously noted ideas are discussed, a new list can be prepared consisting of the qualified ideas that are worth taking to the next level of implementation. The group also may finalize the criterion and indicators that are the yardsticks for achievement. For a problem-solving journey, a brainstorming session may be helpful to finalize the many objectives, to identify the root cause, to prioritize the actions for implementation, and to evaluate investment proposals, if any.

While brainstorming appears to be a good technique, one must be cautious about the shortcomings and limitations that are inherently associated with it. In Table 5.1, various pros and cons are listed to help you understand the benefits and limitations of a structured brainstorming session.

**TABLE 5.1**

Pros and cons of a brainstorming session

| Pros | Cons |
| --- | --- |
| During brainstorming, a variety of new ideas may come up that may help you find better alternatives. | Not all the ideas can be assessed on face value but need sufficient time to be evaluated. |
| Even a person who is naïve in the field may ask a question and propose a point of view that can become a pathfinder. They can help discard conventional ideas. | A native thinker may unilaterally consider one direction that is preconceived and not logically evaluated. Because of this, others may accept their viewpoint without much deliberation. |
| Since all members propose different points of view, even a tough problem may turn out to be an easy one. | |
| The flag-bearer or the leader may be relieved of stress because she may find a shared vision. | At times, brainstorming can be time consuming. Therefore, it may be a deterrent. However, whatever the time constraint, a suitably paced and structured brainstorming session will bring results. |
| A successful session seeks the wisdom of ten people rather than the knowledge of one. | |

## Real Problem-Solving

### SWOT[1] Analysis of a Fortune 500 Company to Aid in a Merger

A subsidiary of a Fortune 500 company is in the final stage of a merger and acquisition deal. The board of directors is tasked to list the various strengths (S), weaknesses (W), opportunities (O), and threats (T) to the organization to present to the new acquiring management. The CEO of the board calls for a brainstorming session to conduct a SWOT analysis.

After the board members gather on time in the designated conference hall, the CEO introduces the issue at hand and explains the objective of the present session. A handout is provided to the board members with all the pertinent information that is important. The team is given 15 minutes to think about and note down any points that they feel are relevant. After this time period is over, the CEO asks the team to speak out one by one about their points. She allows a very short discussion in order to reach the notable points. She also discourages any in-depth discussion about these points.

Throughout this process, she wants to ensure that all thoughts are noted and that none of the items or the thought processes are ignored before they are articulated properly. She conducts the first session in four sub-sessions—for strengths, weaknesses, opportunities, and threats. She notes down all the points that are mentioned at each sub-session. Table 5.2 and Table 5.3 summarize these points.

### TABLE 5.2

Thoughts generated on strengths and weaknesses in the SWOT analysis session

| Strengths | A | Weaknesses | B |
|---|---|---|---|
| 1. Lengthy production experience | √ | 1. Industrial relations | √ |
| 2. Established process system | X | 2. Poor production planning | X |
| 3. Data management technique | X | 3. High cost of production | X |
| 4. Technical know-how | X | 4. Non-availability of low-cost technology | √ |
| 5. Manufacturing flexibility | √ | 5. Problem-solving capability | √ |
| 6. Capacity availability | √ | 6. High employee turnover | √ |
| 7. Durability of product | X | 7. Labor-intensive process | X |
| 8. Brand image and multiple brands | √ | 8. Inability to produce low-cost products | √ |
| 9. Low cost of production | X | 9. Low adaptability to change | √ |
| 10. High productivity index | X | 10. High process throughput time | X |

---

[1] SWOT is an acronym which stands for Strength, Weakness, Opportunity, and Threat.

**TABLE 5.3**

Various thoughts generated on opportunities and threats in the SWOT analysis session

| Opportunities | C | Threats | D |
|---|---|---|---|
| 1. Ever-increasing demand of product | √ | 1. Tough competition | √ |
| 2. Economic growth | √ | 2. Market pressure to reduce price | √ |
| 3. Possibility for exports | √ | 3. Non-availability of critical raw materials | X |
| 4. Adoption of new technology | √ | 4. Environmental issues | X |
| 5. Availability of new breakthrough technology | √ | 5. Brain drain | √ |

During the noting down session, care is taken not to repeat the same point in other ways, which ensures that the noted points are all mutually exclusive. After this first round, the CEO asks for discussion among the board members to reflect upon the various points mentioned regarding strengths, weaknesses, opportunities, and threats. The board members are asked to weigh the various options with respect to the prevalent scenario of the industry and the competition. For example, in Table 5.2, "lengthy production experience" becomes a strength only if the same "lengthy production experience" is not a factor for others in the industry, including the competition. Similarly, "high process throughput time" is not a weakness if "high process throughput time" is common in the industry and for competitors. If the board members agree unanimously on a particular point, they place a tick mark (√), or if they do not agree on a particular point, they place a cross (X) beside the corresponding points in columns A, B, C, and D. The CEO later reduces the lists with the tick marks; she may keep a few other points marked with crosses as well if the team agrees. She ensures that a final copy of the noted points is available for all the members and closes the brainstorming session with her heartfelt thanks. In Tables 5.4 and 5.5, the final discussion output is listed.

**TABLE 5.4**

Short-listed points for strengths and weaknesses of the organization

| Strengths | A | Weaknesses | B |
|---|---|---|---|
| Lengthy production experience | √ | Industrial relations | √ |
| Manufacturing flexibility | √ | Nonavailability of low-cost technology | √ |
| Capacity availability | √ | Problem-solving capability | √ |
| Brand image and multiple brands | √ | High employee turnover | √ |
| | | Inability to produce low-cost products | √ |
| | | Low adaptability to change | √ |

**TABLE 5.5**

Short-listed points for opportunities and threats

| Opportunities | C | Threats | D |
|---|---|---|---|
| 1. Ever-increasing demand of product | √ | 1. Tough competition | √ |
| 2. Economic growth | √ | 2. Market pressure to reduce price | √ |
| 3. Possibility for exports | √ | 3. Brain drain | √ |
| 4. Adoption of new technology | √ | | |
| 5. Availability of new breakthrough technology | √ | | |

If you follow through with this adopted process, you will understand that this activity ensures that all members propose different points of view; therefore, even a tough problem may turn out to be an easy one. This also demonstrates how a successful session seeks the wisdom of ten people rather than the knowledge of one.

## Multi-Voting

Multi-voting, as the name suggests, means multiple voting sessions. Essentially, this is conducted quite a few times in succession to narrow down the primary list that emerges from the team's brainstorming. We have seen in the preceding section about brain storming that, while generating ideas, team members may suggest various options that are both pertinent and important. Although some ideas may not be useful at all. However, pursuing all ideas might become challenging and might not be possible due to time constraints. Therefore, it is important to reduce the length of the first list of priorities and make its size more manageable. In this case, multi-voting may be the solution. This priority-setting tool is also useful for ranking the order of options based on a preset criteria.

---

"Multi-voting is a priority-setting tool that can also be useful for ranking the order of options based on preset criteria."

---

However, if decisions are made with limited discussion, sometimes multi-voting may not yield results. Even though a group of people may make some popular decisions, those may be neither pertinent nor important. Therefore, when using multi-voting, the leader must remain very cautious about its pitfalls. The benefits and limitations of multi-voting are listed in Table 5.6.

Let us now understand the various steps for a multi-voting session. While going through the various steps to conduct a multi-voting session, you will see in Table 5.7 that the activity starts with preparing a large laundry list of issues that may come from an earlier brainstorming session. The next step will be to assign a serial reference number for easy recall. Then voting will

**TABLE 5.6**

Benefits and limitations of multi-voting technique

| Benefits | Limitations |
| --- | --- |
| 1. It is a systematic and noncompetitive process for information generation and decision-making. | 1. Sometimes, the decision may come from a limited discussion. |
| 2. Everyone in the team remains transparent to one another, and everyone feels a part of the process. | 2. The outcome may become unsatisfactory or unacceptable to a majority of team members if it is based simply on voting. |
| 3. It can help sort out a long list of options. | 3. Real issues and important options may not come up for discussion. |

**TABLE 5.7**

Steps to conduct a systematic multi-voting session

| Steps | Description |
| --- | --- |
| Step 1 | Prepare a large laundry list from the earlier brainstorming session. |
| Step 2 | Assign a letter to each item for easy and quick reference. |
| Step 3 | Conduct voting and tally the votes. |
| Step 4 | Repeat voting till the list size reduces to one that is workable. |

be conducted by assigning votes to each member of the team equal to half the number of issues listed. After voting is completed, the votes will be tallied and the list reduced by half. You should repeat the voting procedure till you get a workable number of issues. However, never repeat voting to reduce the options to only one. This will be an error in disguise.

There will be lot of items that are discarded at various stages of voting. Keep all those separately noted as they will be of great interest in future endeavors.

**Real Problem-Solving**

### Why Are the Plates Being Rejected?

In a dinner plate manufacturing company, it was observed that the rejection rate (expressed in percentage of rejected pieces compared to the total pieces produced) of a particular 30-cm-deep bowl is 15.5%, which is extremely high compared to the existing standard in the industry. The executive responsible for the quality assurance function of the production unit calls for a brainstorming session and invites all the heads of the six process stage departments to engage in resolving the issue. The head of the process engineering department acts as a moderator of the session and lists all the relevant points raised by the departmental heads. Each of the various points are assigned a letter (e.g., A, B, and so on) for quick and easy reference as shown in Table 5.8.

**TABLE 5.8**

Laundry list of probable reasons for high rejections in 30-cm luxury dinner plate manufacturing

| | Probable Causes | | Probable Causes |
|---|---|---|---|
| A | The green strength of the product just after the forming process is low. | G | The floor is uneven, so the movement of the trolley is not smooth. |
| B | The temperature gradient in the kiln is high. | H | The rainy season is increasing the atmospheric humidity. |
| C | The operator is new and does not know the machine operation well. | I | Proper handling does not take place during kiln loading. |
| D | One of the raw materials, potassium feldspar, is of inferior quality. | J | The dry strength of the product just after the drying process is low. |
| E | The forming mold temperature is low. | K | One raw material was changed recently and its individual properties are inferior. |
| F | The drier temperature is low, and drying is incomplete. | L | The firing temperature is not sufficient. |

The team used multi-voting to reduce the list size to a workable one. Each of the four members of the team had a maximum of six votes (half of the total 12 issues) to cast for the causes they think are responsible on a scale of "most" to "least." The votes were tallied, and the top six items were selected for the next round of voting. The tally of votes after the first round is summarized in Table 5.9.

In the second round, the top six issues are voted upon. Each of the team members are given three votes to cast (half the number of the

**TABLE 5.9**

Tally of votes after the first round

| | Votes | Probable Causes | | Votes | Probable Causes |
|---|---|---|---|---|---|
| A | III | The green strength of the product just after the forming process is low. | G | I | The floor is uneven, so the movement of the trolley is not smooth. |
| B | IIII | The temperature gradient in the kiln is high. | H | I | The rainy season is increasing the atmospheric humidity. |
| C | II | The operator is new and does not know the machine operation well. | I | III | Proper handling does not take place during kiln loading. |
| D | I | One of the raw materials, potassium feldspar, is of inferior quality. | J | I | The green strength of the product just after the drying process is low. |
| E | III | The forming mold temperature is low. | K | II | One raw material was changed recently and its individual properties are inferior. |
| F | II | The drier temperature is low, and drying is incomplete. | L | I | The firing temperature is not sufficient. |

**TABLE 5.10**

Tally of votes after the second round

| | Votes | Probable causes | | Votes | Probable causes |
|---|---|---|---|---|---|
| A | III | The green strength of the product just after the forming process is low. | F | II | The drier temperature is low and drying is incomplete. |
| | | | I | I | Proper handling does not take place during kiln loading. |
| B | I | The temperature gradient in the kiln is high. | K | III | One raw material was changed recently and its individual properties are inferior. |
| E | II | The forming mold temperature is low. | | | |

total 6 issues). The votes are tallied, and the top three items are selected for initiating immediate action. The tally after the second round of voting is provided in Table 5.10. The number of votes cast in the second round is in the column headed "Votes."

After the second vote tally, the team decides to work on the three major issues and a fourth one that the team decides to investigate further to determine which issues affect the rate of rejection the most: (a) The green strength of the product just after the forming process is low; (b) one raw material was changed recently and its individual properties are inferior; (c) the drier temperature is low, and drying is incomplete; and (d) the forming mold temperature is low.

As a result of the multi-voting exercise, after thoughtful deliberations, the team could arrive at workable options to initiate actions for problem-solving and improvement.

## Tools for Generating Ideas and Organizing Basic Information

### Affinity Diagrams

The affinity diagram is constructed when different potential causes can be attributed to an effect [2]. These are more common in complex situations, and there can be multiple possibilities.

Generally, this tool is used after a brainstorming activity to sort and write down a large quantity of ideas and opinions in several groups of logical sequence that allow alignments of thoughts for better understanding of the situation and planning future actions. The elements in the diagram may or may not have causal relationships, but they eventually help in further analysis and better identification and understanding of causes and effects. This, in turn, helps in planning future actions.

In a multidisciplinary problem scenario, where it is envisaged that there can be multiple causes with various partial contributions of different priorities or

**TABLE 5.11**

How to construct an affinity diagram

| Serial # | Steps for Construction | Remark: Procedure or Sources or Outcome |
|---|---|---|
| 1 | Identify and state the subject for the team members. | The topic may come from a customer complaint or any other quality review. |
| 2 | Generate a long list of ideas from different sources. | The sources may be a list of customer complaints received, workers' interviews, or the results from a brainstorming session. |
| 3 | Distribute Post-it® sticky notes to all team members and advise them to write all their ideas on these notes. | It is mandatory to write only one idea on one note. |
| 4 | Review all the notes and try to figure out a few basic section headings for ideas. | Group these headings. |
| 5 | Arrange the notes with similar ideas under one section. | Similar ideas should be arranged under the same group heads as per their relationships. |
| 6 | Give each section a heading. | Arrange headings in a logical sequence. |

importance, multiple teams may be deployed to find answers. The teams can organize their ideas and opinions in an affinity diagram. In this way, ideas from every member can be documented in a structured manner.

"Affinity diagrams may pinpoint the real problem situation in a state of confusion. This is a creative process. Many times creativity gives a new dimension to the issue under consideration."

In Table 5.11, a few simple steps are listed for easy understanding and indicates that after the subject matter is identified, the next step in the process will be to list all the potential ideas on Post-it®[2] sticky notes. When reviewing all the notes gathered, a major task will be to find out some major groups into which the ideas can be assembled. Then similar ideas can be placed under group headings for better understanding.

The outcome of the affinity diagram is a list of various actionable ideas under a group subheading that has a strong relationship with the apex problem identified at the beginning.

## CRITICAL THINKING QUESTION

After going through the characteristics of the affinity diagram, can you think of any other scenario, not mentioned here, where techniques of preparing an affinity diagram can be employed successfully?

---

[2] Post-it® notes are small paper scraps with "low-tack," reusable, pressure-sensitive adhesive, originally patented by 3M.

**Real Problem-Solving**

## Implementing an Organization-Wide Structured Problem-Solving Approach

The management of a continuous process plant has decided to implement an organization-wide structured problem-solving approach for all quality and productivity related issues. However, after the initial kickoff, it was observed that the employees are not very energized about the new approach, and it is becoming a challenge to implement a structured work method. Upon investigation, the teams may construct an affinity diagram for the issues faced when implementing a structured problem-solving approach in everyday work.

The team discusses the issue among themselves and with other team members on the shop floor. They generate a lot of probable reasons for the challenge of implementing a new approach in problem-solving. They write these on Post-its® and paste them on a wall. In Figure 5.1, we find a few of the points listed by the team members.

After the initial listing, the team then reviews all the points and decides on some group headings such as (a) implementation issues,

| | | |
|---|---|---|
| People are reluctant to change. | People are habituated to the waste in the process, and they are not aware of the risks due to this waste. | People are happy working in their domains and are not ready to open up. |
| There is a lack of management focus. | | Training, rewards and recognition are lacking. |
| Sharing of information about the new process is not done satisfactorily. | Proper implementation is lacking. | |
| A proper system is lacking. | There is a lack of basic training among the workers. | Concepts are not easy to use. |
| People are less involved. | There is lack of benchmarking. | The new approach is thought to be more time consuming. |
| The new approach will increase everyone's work content. | There is a lack of interest in learning about a new subject. | |

**FIGURE 5.1**
List of ideas concerning the challenges faced when implementing a new structured approach to problem-solving.

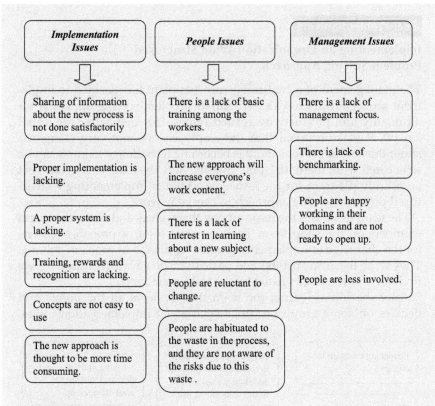

**FIGURE 5.2**
Resultant affinity diagram after review of organizational issues.

(b) management issues, and (c) people issues. The team members then try to group all the similar points under each heading. The resultant list is shown in Figure 5.2.

After this stage, the team may once again start a discussion to identify various actionable points to mitigate the issues depicted in the affinity diagram. A multi-voting session may be conducted to reduce the number of actionable points. For every issue short-listed in the affinity diagram, a brainstorming session may be initiated to find the root cause to further understand the actions.

## Tree Diagram

A tree diagram is an analytical diagram that depicts a hierarchical structure [3]. This diagram starts with a single point, item, or node and moves one step at a time, spreading out into branches. For instance, when we toss a coin, there are two possible outcomes—either heads or tails, both of which are

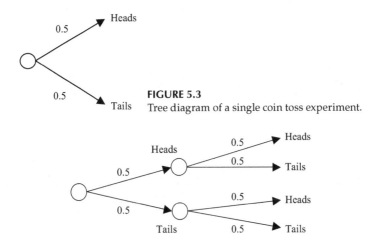

**FIGURE 5.3**
Tree diagram of a single coin toss experiment.

**FIGURE 5.4**
Tree diagram with probable outcome of a successive coin toss experiment.

equally likely. Though these probabilities do not ensure what the outcome of the next toss will be, they do tell us what is *likely* to happen. Because the outcome can be either heads or tails in a single toss, the probability of turning up heads or tails is 0.5. This outcome can be represented by a simple diagram as depicted in Figure 5.3.

If the same coin toss experiment continued further, the subsequent outcomes can be expressed as in Figure 5.4.

This tree diagram gives us a visual interpretation of various outcomes that are likely to happen. The concept of a tree diagram can also be used to determine in successive detail the various possibilities of failure. This type of analysis may be helpful in finding the root cause of a problem. Also, during a brainstorming session, the discussion outcome may be documented for a quick visual understanding.

"A tree diagram is also helpful in locating the flaws, deficiencies, or incompetence in the source data. The tree diagram helps differentiate the specifics from generalities."

**Real Problem-Solving**

**Why Does the Generator Fail to Start?**

Let us use an engineering example to illustrate the concept further in real life. In a mechanical workshop, an electric generator is not working and fails to start. During the analysis phase, various causes surface.

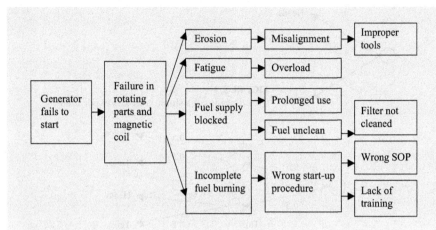

**FIGURE 5.5**
Tree diagram of plausible causes for a generator failing to start.

Some have a direct and some have an indirect causal relationship to the problem of the generator not working. Observe closely how the dependent causal relationships are detailed in Figure 5.5.

It is evident that each branch in the tree diagram represents a probable outcome; in this case, a reason for the preceding issue is mentioned when the diagram is read from left to right. This diagram helps one to systematically write down thoughts in progression and assists one in finding out the root cause of the problem.

Thus, a tree diagram helps us systematically enlist the outcomes from a random discussion. There are horizontal or even vertical tree diagrams. The basic idea is to branch out the ideas into subsequent stages.

## SIPOC Diagram

SIPOC is an acronym for supplier, input, process, output, and customer [4, 5]. This diagram is a part of a high-level process diagram. As the single words indicate, all the steps are included here from the supplier to the customer. A SIPOC diagram is used to visualize the overall business process of an

## CRITICAL THINKING QUESTION

Pause for a while and think for a moment. Can you think of any limitation of this technique that may hinder the quality of outcome of the tree diagram making process?

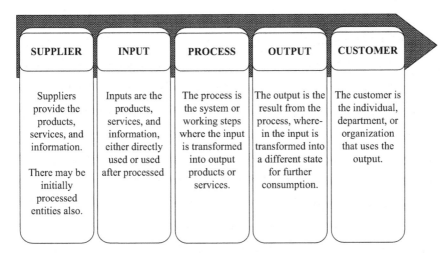

**FIGURE 5.6**
Various elements of a SIPOC diagram.

organization. If a nonconformity arises, a SIPOC diagram helps in identifying the possible location of the problem and in identifying the solutions.

These diagrams show us the limits and boundaries of the major and important processes but do not deal with much detail. Therefore, the big picture is never lost. This diagram is useful when it is important to focus on the discussion to reach a common understanding of the process. Figure 5.6 defines this further.

Examples of "suppliers" may be departments, a business office, staff, government, or professionals. The input can be data, knowledge, resources, or a precursor to the problem. This depends on the system we are analyzing.

We may recall that the "suppliers" may be internal or external, and the same is true for "customers." Similarly, in a closed loop internal process, the same customers may become suppliers for the next SIPOC analysis. A SIPOC diagram challenges the problem-solver/team to consider all elements of the "system" while setting clear boundaries of where the project starts and where the project stops in terms of overall scope of work. In real life SIPOC analysis Post-It notes are used to note down the ideas and are pasted in respective heads. This is to facilitate easy removal and editing if required.

---

"SIPOC is a high-level process diagram that challenges the problem-solver/team to consider all elements of the 'system' while setting clear boundaries of where the project starts and where the project stops."

---

Building on the definition mentioned here, an everyday example will help to elaborate the concept further.

### Real Problem-Solving

### SIPOC with Finance

Imagine you are on a trekking expedition with your fiancé. On a cool autumn evening, two of you are resting beside a narrow mountain stream. She suggests having a cup of hot cowboy coffee.[3] Let us see how the entire process can be converted into a SIPOC diagram as depicted in Figure 5.7.

As you may observe, a mundane job of preparing a cup of coffee is analyzed with a structured approach that reveals all the finite elements involved in it. However, in a real-life situation, preparing and enjoying a fresh cup of coffee would be preferable to doing a SIPOC analysis!

| Supplier | Input | Process | Output | Customer |
|---|---|---|---|---|
| Coffee | Sufficient | Grind coffee beans ↓ | Delicious | Your fiancé, beside |
| store | water | Add water to pot ↓ | cowboy coffee | the campfire |
| | Coffee beans | Heat it to boiling ↓ | in a warm | Your business partner |
| | Coffeepot | Allow to cool to 80°C ↓ | porcelain cup | yourself |
| | Stove/campfire | Add 2 TBSP of coffee and stir ↓ | | |
| | Porcelain cups | Allow 2 minutes to age ↓ | | |
| | | Mildly stir again ↓ | | |
| | | Allow 2 minutes to age ↓ | | |
| | | Slowly pour coffee to cup | | |

**FIGURE 5.7**
SIPOC diagram for preparation of cowboy coffee, an illustrative example.

---

[3] Cowboy coffee is an occasionally terrible coffee that is made only using ground beans, water, whatever pot is around, and a campfire; it does not necessarily contain any milk and sugar.

### Process Flow Chart

A process is a chain of steps where input is converted to output [5]. The output may become input for the next process in subsequent steps. There are two others terms associated with a process. These are "suppliers" and "customers." The input to the process comes from the suppliers and the output of a process goes to a customer. The simple diagram in Figure 5.8 explains this aspect.

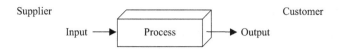

**FIGURE 5.8**
Location of a process in the entire operational cycle.

The schematic in Figure 5.8 tells us the position of the process stages in reference to the related stakeholders, as mentioned earlier in the SIPOC diagram. A typical process map is a graphical representation of steps, events, operations, and resource relationships within a process. In order to understand a process better, we have to know the elements of the process as detailed in the schematic of the basic flow chart in Figure 5.9.

There are a few other symbols that are used in specific depictions of flow charts. The curious reader may consult some of the reference books on this subject.

## Cause and Effect Diagram

This is a very simple tool that is used to investigate the possible causes of a problem in a very structured manner [6]. The inherent construction of this diagram forces one to think in such a manner. This diagram enumerates the various potential causes that result from the effects. It also illustrates the hierarchy of causes, wherein it is shown that the causes have causes and those in turn have causes and so on. The classical diagram resembles the full body bone structure of a fish. Therefore, this diagram is also called a fishbone diagram. This simple tool was first used and popularized by Kaoru Ishikawa[4] in the 1940s. Therefore, this diagram is also called an Ishikawa diagram. Figure 5.10 is a schematic of an Ishikawa diagram showing the basic elements of the structure.

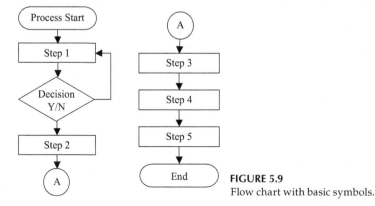

**FIGURE 5.9**
Flow chart with basic symbols.

[4] https://en.wikipedia.org/wiki/Kaoru_Ishikawa

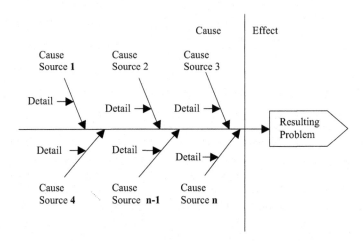

**FIGURE 5.10**
Structure of a cause and effect diagram.

Considerable thought has been given to this concept of cause and effect analysis. In different organizations, there must be various cause sources that are typical of these organizations. Research shows that various causes can be grouped into sets of four or five common sources of causes that encompass all the different areas. Therefore, the most important cause sources may be summarized using the acronym 4Ms. These are man, machine, method, and material. Sometimes as a complimentary addendum, two new cause sources are added—mother (for the environment) and measurements. The details that are to be identified must be mutually exclusive for all the cause sources. Next we will discuss the fundamental details of these well-established sources.

The cause source *man* refers to all the causes that are initiated, activated, and/or undertaken by an individual manually. These causes result from human interference. Examples may include lack of focus, lack of sleep, lack of skill, and even excessive traveling, and so on.

The cause source *machine* refers to all the causes that are generated from machines or, in some cases, the tools used to deliver services. Therefore, when a cause originates directly from a machine and not from the use of a machine, it might be addressed here. If the cause originates from the use of a machine, then it might be included either in *man* (for skill) or *method* (for process).

The cause source *method* refers to the processes followed to generate defects/effects by the addition of contributions from *man* and *machine*. Examples may include lack of documentation, slow flow of communication due to the use of the postal system, lack of an alert system for the employees to react in time, insufficient training, and so on. Care must be taken not to assign the causes related to *methods* to both *man* and *machine*.

The cause source *material* refers to the input materials for the process. For the manufacturing sector, examples may include poor or insufficient design, substandard raw materials, flow of incomplete in-process materials, and so on.

---

"The cause and effect diagram can be used in any situation, and it does not require any prior knowledge of statistics or mathematics."

---

While preparing the cause and effect diagram, care must be taken to attribute a cause to the proper source heading. This clarity will help team members focus on identification of correct causes.

Different industries have different sets of cause centers. These are mostly predefined and have been very well researched. A brief summary of the cause centers in various sectors are enumerated in Table 5.12.

The widely applied cause and effect diagram is very important and is useful for determining various potential causes and thereby finding a problem's root cause. Causes may be documented in various ways; however, a typical pictorial presentation displays a systematic data flow that can be followed and reviewed easily. A lateral flow diagram also takes advantage of the usual writing direction of left to right.

This tool can also be used to write down thoughts in a structured way while a team is brainstorming. Usually this diagram is created as a result of a brainstorming session in a large group and in a small group. It is observed that in the midst of a brainstorming session, the participants come up with various ideas that sometimes are contradictory to one another. Noting all of the ideas in the same place becomes an increasingly tougher challenge. Moreover, the challenge becomes out of control when the team size increases to more than ten participants and when the team is made up of different participants with different types of responsibilities. Arranging the ideas in a systematic order becomes a real challenge.

**TABLE 5.12**

Elements of cause and effect diagram in various sectors

| Manufacturing Sector | Service Sector | Administration/Marketing Wings |
|---|---|---|
| 6M | 4S | 8P |
| Manpower | Surroundings | Product (or service) |
| Machines | Suppliers | Price |
| Methods | Systems | People |
| Materials | Skills | Place |
| Measurement | | Promotion |
| Mother (environment) | | Procedures/Policies |

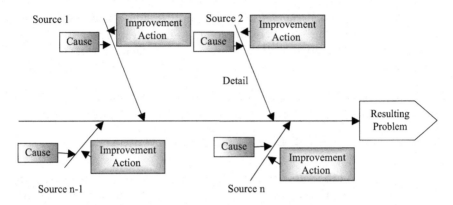

**FIGURE 5.11**
Schematic cause and effect diagram with additions of cards (CEDAC).

In order to get rid of these kinds of challenges, in the 1970s, Dr. Ryuji Fukuda[5] developed an improved process whereby a cause and effect discussion is conducted with the participants writing their opinions on cards, and these cards are pasted on paper. The cards are then removed and reposted as they are reassigned to different cause lines. This is called a cause and effect diagram with the addition of cards, or CEDAC [7]. This tool helps large groups brainstorm and systematically collect, analyze, and integrate information for problem-solving and improvement.

As an extension of the traditional fishbone diagram, when developing a CEDAC, a large skeletal arrow structure is drawn on a very large piece of paper (it may be size A0 or double that) pasted on a wall. In Figure 5.11, a simple schematic CEDAC is displayed for easy comprehension. Instead of writing directly on the paper, the participants write the probable causes on Post-it® notes and paste them on the left side of the suitable arrow. To express a better causal relationship, these Post-it® notes can be relocated to different arrow positions, similar to creating an affinity diagram. After sufficient causes are identified, the participants may again hold a discussion and find some factors for improvement. Participants write these points of improvement on Post-it® notes and paste them on the right-hand side of the arrows beside the respective causes. In a real-life scenario, this CEDAC will be more helpful for noting down improvement action plans while free-flow brainstorming with operators and workers in a larger team.

After the preliminary cause and improvement actions are noted, the teams may have another joint discussion and use a three-dot system to assign a status to the work or to the results of improvement actions.

These two kinds of cards, the fact or problem cards (pasted on the left of the arrow line) and the solution or improvement cards (pasted on the right

---

[5] https://it.wikipedia.org/wiki/Ryuji_Fukuda

of the arrow line) ensure that the facts and the probable improvement points are collected and organized before solutions are actually tested or implemented. The probable solutions are then selected through a process of thorough discussion and evaluated. The statuses of the probable solutions are noted on the effect side using this three dot system. The established convention for this three dot system is as follows

a. One dot (•): the idea is of interest;

b. two dots (••): the idea is under the preparation; and

c. Three dots (•••): the idea is under the test.

In a typical CADAC exercise Post-It cards of darker color are used for the cause-line on the left and lighter colors are used for the improvement-action-line on the right. This is to easily identify and facilitate relocation of ideas, if required.

One of the major advantages of using a cause and effect diagram is that it allows us to write down all the ideas concurrently, which also improves the team spirit. A few examples of cause and effect diagrams will help us understand the subject.

## Real Problem-Solving

### A Day in the Logistics Department of Allied Chemical Products

As per the three-sector theory, the economic sectors are subdivided into three major parts. These are the raw material sector (the primary sector), the manufacturing sector (the secondary sector), and the service sector (the tertiary sector). The end product of the service sector is service. Services are essentially intangible goods that include, inter alia, transportation, distribution, access, advice, attention and experience, effective labor to bring about the intended experience for consumer, and health care.

The newly formed Allied Chemical Products company has been receiving repeated customer complaints about delayed supply of goods. The organization's management has been tasked with finding the various reasons for the delay. The team conducts a brainstorming session and notes down all the possible causes into subgroups of man, method, measurement, mother/environment, material, and machine, in a very structured manner resulting in a cause and effects diagram. Figure 5.12 summarizes all the possible causes.

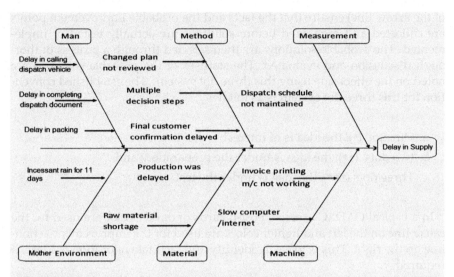

**FIGURE 5.12**
Cause and effect diagram of a delay in the supply of goods.

Figure 5.12 shows how, in the manufacturing sector, six groups of causes such as man, method, measurement, mother/environment, material, and machine can contribute to delays in supplying goods to customers.

## Real Problem-Solving

### "Bend It Like Banana" Failed to Score at the Box Office

Mr. Nicolas Heisenberg produced a movie named "Bend It Like Banana" based on the true life story of a famous soccer player from Uruguay. The story was inspiring, and the script was written by one of Hollywood's best script writers. The director had been nominated for an Oscar three times. However, the movie fared very poorly on opening day, and box office sales were pathetic. Mr. Heisenberg wants to find the reason for this debacle. He engages you to look into the matter and to find out the root cause of this failure. Quite a lot of intense thinking and several brainstorming sessions results in a cause and effect diagram, as depicted in Figure 5.13, that you will present to the board of investors.

The probable causes in Figure 5.13 are left intentionally blank. As a creative problem-solver and a resourceful reader, would you like to give this a try? Would you like to try conducting a brainstorming session among your fellow friends to find out the influential causes that

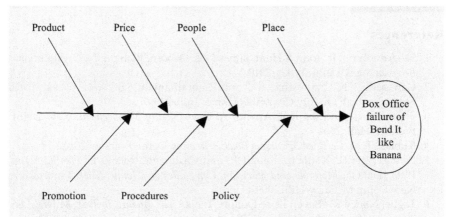

**FIGURE 5.13**
Probable cause groups for failure of the movie "Bend It Like Banana."

might have resulted in the failure of the movie, "Bend It Like Banana"? While you conduct the session, you may assume a few of the most obvious causes that are true and go ahead.

### Review Questions

1. Discuss with example the properties of a fruitful brainstorming session. Enlist dos and donts for conducting a successful brainstorming session.

2. Discuss in detail the process of conducting a multi-voting session.

3. Critically think and list some of the merits and demerits of multi-voting techniques.

4. Discuss how an affinity diagram help a team prioritize the issues and help pinpoint a real problem situation in a state of confusion.

5. Discuss with example how the tree diagram can help us locate flaws or defiencies in the source of data.

6. SIPOC is a high level process diagram. Take an example of the business process that you are dealing in and prepare a detailed SIPOC diagram.

7. Prepare a process flow chart of any of the processes in the manufacturing or service industry you are working. Critically evaluate all the small process steps and discuss how they contribute to the overall outcome of the process.

8. Enumerate the benefits of CEDAC process while trying to prepare a cause and effect diagram towards finding the root cause of a problem.

## References

1. Schermerhorn, Jr., John R Hunt, James G. & Osborn, Richard, N. *Organizational Behavior*. New Delhi: Wiley, 2010.
2. Ganapathy, K, Narayana, V., and Subramaniam, B. *New Seven Tools*. Secunderabad: Quality Council Forum of India, 1997.
3. Sugandhi, L. and Samuel, Anand, A. *Total Quality Management*. New Delhi: Prentice-Hall, 2004.
4. Kubiak, T. M. *Certified Six Sigma Black Belt*. New Delhi: Pearson, 2010.
5. Pande, Peter S., Neuman, Robert P., and Cavanagh, Roland R. *The Six Sigma Way: How GE, Motorola, and other Top Companies are Honing Their Performance*, New Delhi: McGraw-Hill, 2009.
6. Tague, Nancy R. "Seven Basic Quality Tools." *The Quality Toolbox*. Milwaukee: American Society for Quality, 2004.
7. Fukuda, Ryuji. *CEDAC: A Tool for Continuous Systematic Improvement*. Boca Raton, FL: Productivity Press, 1996.

WHEN GOWRIE MET KRISHNA:

*Gowrie:* I am fed up. When will I solve this problem?
*Krishna:* You can't solve the problem until you start asking the right questions.

# 6

## Techniques and Tools for Collecting Data and Collating Information

If I had 20 days to solve a problem, I would take 19 days to define it.

**Albert Einstein**

### Objectives

After going through this chapter and understanding the issues described in it, you will be able to deal more efficiently with the challenges in problem-solving:

1. *Understand* the basic techniques for collecting and collating information.
2. *Weigh* the voice of customers to understand real feedback.
3. *Compile* meaningful check sheets.
4. *Develop* matrix diagrams for interdependent issues with multidisciplinary parameters.

### Chapter at a Glance

In this chapter, we will discuss various techniques and tools for collecting and collating information in a very structured manner for a fruitful journey ahead. Techniques like sampling and capturing the voice of customers, even more than the data and information, are very important because their quick and easy recall is vital for all succeeding steps in problem-solving. Here, the word "customers" does not necessarily mean the end customers alone; they may well be internal customers who use products from previous sections of the operation. For greater understanding, we also will discuss simple tools, such as often-used check sheets and customized tools such as matrix diagrams. The case studies in the real problem-solving section will help you further understand the application of these techniques and tools in real life.

## Techniques for Collecting Data and Collating Information

### Sampling

In an industrial or professional setup, once ideas are generated and basic information is collected for a nonconformity or a problem, the next activity would be to collect more data for further analysis. In order to resolve issues, we need to conduct planned experiments; therefore, an assortment of data is required. Samples are used to keep a constant vigil on the output parameters, so it becomes very important to identify the quality, quantity, and frequency of samples to be collected that represent the entire population.

"To represent the entire population, it will be very important to identify the quality, quantity, and frequency of samples to be collected."

A sample is a small collection of a larger population of products, process parameters or even services [1]. The samples are examined and data from the desired parameters are collected. Based on the collected data, we need to make inferences about the entire population. However, variations naturally occur. Therefore, we have to be careful to select the samples in such a way that they contain the target parameters in the same density as in the population. For the variations that are inherent, this will be simple. Because of these variations, the successive samples of any continuous manufacturing process will differ. Therefore, a certain characteristic of a sample may not be representative of the entire population.

### Real Problem-Solving

### Why Do Rough Edges Appear in the Stainless Steel Tumblers?

Consider a continuous manufacturing operation, where stainless steel tumblers are produced. Of late, the quality assurance department has received quite a few market complaints about tumblers having rough edges to the tune of 0.06%. This is calculated on the basis of dividing the number of complaints received by the total number of tumblers dispatched in the same period. The process control team has received some pieces with rough edges as defect samples. On initial investigation, it is understood that the complaints are from different areas of the country. Therefore, it is expected that the products are not from the same lot produced all at one time but are from different lots produced at different points of time. The team wants to identify the pieces in the production process itself, and they decide to check products before packing and dispatch. The occurrence rate of the defects is 0.06%. This means that there are six pieces out of every 10,000 pieces that are faulty and are attracting complaints. Here, the investigator has to decide on a sampling process and size so that the sample group contains defective tumblers.

### Real Problem-Solving

#### How Did the Movie Fare at the Box Office?

Consider another example of collecting information about a new movie being shown in town. You are tasked with obtaining feedback about the movie's story line, actors, and actresses. You decide to take a random sample of 15 people's opinions by interviewing moviegoers when they come out of the theater after watching the film. Suppose, you now decide to watch the movie yourself along with your family members and some distant relatives. If you pick only your family members and the people who are sitting in your vicinity, this sample survey will not constitute the opinion of the entire population and will not really serve the original purpose of the task.

Therefore, you as a problem-solver are confronted with twin challenges: to design, schedule, and conduct the sampling in such a way that the collected samples should represent the entire population and then, after the samples are studied, to make inferences that are appropriate for initiating actions. For proper sampling, it will be important for you to adhere to a few guidelines.

1. Investigate and clarify the quantity and frequency of the samples.
2. Decide the tolerance and identify the correct time for sampling.
3. Ensure randomness while collecting the samples.
4. Record any process abnormality during the sampling activity.
5. Record other interrelated information together with the desired parameter in the sample.
6. Check whether necessary samples are collected, and check again for sufficiency.

## Voice of the Customer

The voice of the customer essentially is the feedback from the various sections of users, which may include internal process customers who are part of the succeeding steps of the process or the end users for whom the product or the process actually are designed [2]. This is a term that often is used in industrial problem-solving as well as in other spheres of business and operations. Other than mainly collecting data and information from customers about their experiences and expectations when using products and services, capturing the voice of the customers is a very effective and quick technique for collecting information on the problems those customers face.

Knowing the voice of the customer remains very important with regard to how the product or the process is doing. Is it really serving the purpose it is designed for? Does the product require any improvement? Does it require frequent repair or replacement? Is it offering the user a value for their money? This voice can also act as a probable lead in solving various problems. Both the internal and external customers contribute immensely to the collection of information.

Capturing the voice of the customer requires a very thorough approach in order to be specific to the real requirements of the user. A structured approach in capturing the voice of customers would help a problem-solver organize the information, plan the required actions, and schedule the implementation in a systematic manner. The process of capturing the voice of customers is described in brief in Figure 6.1.

Customer information from both internal and external sources can be solicited or sometimes unsolicited. This type of information can be either routine or random in nature. Based on the type of information, feedback can also be either quantitative or qualitative. Depending upon the source of the

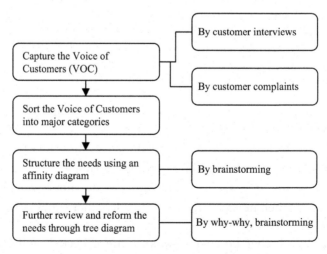

**FIGURE 6.1**
Capturing the voice of customers—the process in brief.

**TABLE 6.1**

Types of information for the voice of the customer—sources and possible uses

| Types | | Unsolicited Information | | Solicited Information | |
|---|---|---|---|---|---|
| | | Routine | Random | Routine | Random |
| Qualitative Information | Use | Real, unbiased situation revealed | Defects and weaknesses | Understanding choices and preferences | Redirect the firm's progress in desired path |
| | Source | Public meetings, grapevine | Meetings, vendors, downstream product users | Purpose-based groups | Exhibitions, consultants |
| Quantitative Information | Use | Help evaluate the performance of the offering | Status of the product, positioning | Learning from mistakes | Status in the users' base |
| | Source | Customer surveys, market surveys, channel trials | Research reports, public reports | Tech journals, business magazines | Warranty claims, notices, market complaints |

information, the type and the use may vary as well. In Table 6.1, we find a summary of such varied information.

The customer needs are captured through recording the customers' voice either by interviewing them or understanding their complaints about the products, processes, or the services offered to them. After the entire laundry list is noted, we will sort the needs according to some gross subdivisions so as to be able to address similar issues in a similar manner. We may also create groups according to the gravity of the situation. While mitigating the problems and complaints, a few questions should be kept in mind in order to undertake a sustainable and successful problem-solving journey. These questions are summarized as follows.

- How important is the customer's need?
- Is this a standalone need or would all customers need this?
- How are we geared up to meet this need?
- Are the resource available for doing so?
- How are others satisfying customer needs under similar conditions?
- How does this need compare other similar needs?

Once the groups are created, the next job will be to create an affinity diagram so that the interrelationships of the needs are understood. The team may use various techniques such as brainstorming to arrive at the desired level of clarity. For further paring down of the needs toward a workable solution, the team may decide to run a why-why analysis to arrive at a tree diagram to determine the fundamental reasons why the customers have complaints.

## Tools for Collecting Data and Collating Information

### Check Sheets

Check sheets are documents one uses to record various types of input and to check whether that input has been adhered to, complied with, or is just available at the problem area. In an everyday scenario, we use check sheets, an example of which could be a list of items available on a restaurant's breakfast menu, a list of pupils who arrived at school with their sweatshirts on, a list of taxpayers who have paid the taxes before the due date, and so on. The appropriate list will provide indications of when is the right occasion to use it.

Check sheets can help in documenting structured data sets in the problem-solving journey. The structured data will always provide us with clear directions during analysis. There are various occasions when check sheets can be used. A few examples are listed here.

a. When manual data are to be entered into a program
b. When it is necessary to collect, count, and classify data for further analysis
c. When there are multiple entries and it is necessary to assign them to specific subsections (i.e., to classify them)
d. When it is necessary to check the distribution of data over a large span

How the check sheets can be used effectively is demonstrated in the following examples of different situations. For mastering the use of this tool, one has to use it as much as possible. Careful thinking before designing a check sheet will surely yield good results.

**Real Problem-Solving**

## Checking Components for Multiple Defects

In order to check the quality of the anti-corrosion coating of metal-oxide composite components, a typical check sheet prepared by the quality control engineers is depicted in Figure 6.2. This type of check sheet is used when a set of products is examined for nonconformities and where there are multiple defects in one product.

| Component: [Name of component] = | | Date: |
|---|---|---|
| Coating booth: [location of the defect generation] : | | |
| Recipe:_____ | | |
| No. of components checked: ___Operator signature:_____ | | |
| Defects | Count | No |
| Low Thickness | IIIII  IIIII  IIIII II | 17 |
| Bubble | IIIII   II | 7 |
| Pin holes | II | 2 |
| Face Holes | I | 1 |
| Extraneous Dirt | I | 1 |
| Carbon Contamination | | 0 |

**FIGURE 6.2**
Checklist for defect counting for metal oxide components.

**Real Problem-Solving**

## Check Sheet of Defects with Reference to its Location in a Consumer Product

In this type of check sheet, as presented in Table 6.2, the probable defects are listed in Column 1 (C1), along with the possible locations on the horizontal axis, as in C2 to C5. A provision for the sum total is also provided in C6.

This check sheet displays how many of the various defects are distributed throughout the product.

**TABLE 6.2**

Check sheet format for location-wise defects in an amorphous display glass product

| Column 1 | C2 | C3 | C4 | C5 | C6 |
|---|---|---|---|---|---|
| Defects/Locations | A | B | C | D | Total |
| Cord | I | II | I | | 4 |
| Cat Scratch | | | II | | 2 |
| Dent | | II | | III | 5 |
| Bubble | I | | | | 1 |
| Total defects | 2 | 4 | 3 | 3 | 12 |

## Real Problem-Solving

### Check Sheet for Design Review

For a new product design process, there are a few fundamental steps for conducting the first design review before the new product design starts. This check sheet ensures that all the preliminary important meetings and discussions occurred and that the minimum required information for arriving at the new product's specifications is captured. It also helps capture other information such as the date when this occurred, and an update of the status of the work. In Table 6.3, a checklist is provided that can be used for the first design review process before the real new product development starts. It should be noted that there is no information on CTQ.[1] It only ensures that the meetings are conducted.

**TABLE 6.3**

Checklist for first design review ensuring the necessary information is captured

| Sl No | Aspects | Date | Status |
|---|---|---|---|
| 1 | Customer requirement documentation is complete | xxx | *** |
| 2 | Product use essentials are documented | xxx | *** |
| 3 | Customer–Designer discussion took place | xxx | *** |
| 4 | Product specifications are captured | xxx | *** |
| 5 | Process requirements are documented | xxx | *** |
| 6 | Identification of CTQ parameters completed. | | |

---

[1] CTQ: Critical to quality. (This refers to the parameters of the product that are vital for quality of performance and final product acceptance.)

### Real Problem-Solving

## Check Sheet for the Occurrence of Particular Diseases at a Construction Site

On construction sites, workers usually stay in conditions that are not that good or are not healthy. As a result, there is an abundance of common disease that may sometimes become deadly and cause havoc. The child mortality rate is also high. In order to find out the frequency of occurrence of various diseases, all the common symptoms are listed. While investigating the frequency of various ailments prevalent among the workers, a check sheet is prepared to capture some relevant data. From the check sheet, Table 6.4 is created, which only shows the occurrence of symptoms among workers at a temporary construction site from January to December 2015.

This table derived from the primary checklist shows a trend, and one may easily see that Frida J. suffered from frequent spells of cough and cold during the year investigated.

**TABLE 6.4**

Frequency of occurrence of various disease symptoms among young workers

| Sl No | Name | Code | Common Cold and Cough | Body Ache | Fever | Nausea & Vomiting |
|-------|------|------|-----------------------|-----------|-------|-------------------|
| 1 | Thomas B. | 957 | 6 | 2 | 2 | 3 |
| 2 | Cathy E. | 089 | 9 | 6 | 2 | 2 |
| 3 | Frida J. | 657 | 13 | 7 | 9 | 5 |
| 4 | Abram S. | 234 | 2 | 2 | 0 | 0 |

## Matrix Diagram

As the name suggests, a matrix diagram is constructed to depict various elements and their interrelationship. Unlike a tree diagram, which shows a direct cause and effect relationship, a matrix diagram indicates the interdependence of various units or parameters [3]. In a typical matrix for a manufacturing setup, unit operations critical to quality are listed against attributes that are critical to quality. A CT[2] matrix that is obtained would look like that provided in Table 6.5. Various parameters that are *critical to the process* of production (CTP[3] as CTP1, CTP2... and so on) are listed along the vertical column heads, and the parameters that are *critical to the quality* of the product (CTQ[4]s as CTQ1, CTQ2...and so on) are listed as the horizontal heads. The interrelationships between the parameters that are *critical to quality* and the parameters that are *critical to production* are characterized as strong, moderate, and weak; their respective symbols are a rhombus, triangle, and circle, respectively. The quality and process parameters can be in any one of the table axes.

In a process study, during a problem-solving journey, the preparation of a matrix diagram can be very useful. Let us use a real-world example to illustrate the concept further.

**TABLE 6.5**

A CT matrix to display the relative importance of critical-to-process and critical-to-quality parameters

|        | CTP1 | CTP2 | CTP3 | CTP4 |
|--------|------|------|------|------|
| CTQ1   | ◇    | ◯    | ◇    | ◯    |
| CTQ2   | △    | ◯    | ◯    | △    |
| CTQ3   | ◯    | ◇    | △    | ◯    |
| CTQ4   | ◯    | ◯    | △    | ◯    |

---

[2] CT Stands for 'Critical To', as in Critical To Process (CTP).
[3] CTP: Critical to process or production.
[4] CTQ = critical to quality.

**Real Problem-Solving**

## How Skimmed Milk Powder is Manufactured

In the milk powder production process, there are various parameters that control the output quality of the milk powder. The production process involves spraying milk in a chamber with a hot air flow inside. The sprayed milk droplets are dried and the powder thus generated is accumulated and conveyed to storage bins. There are 11 fundamental process parameters that control the production output. For easy understanding, five different output parameters such as granulometry (the grain size distribution of the dry milk grains expressed in fractions of millimeters), residual moisture (%), production output rate (kg per hour), accumulation of finer particles in the exhaust system (kg per hour), and temperature of the output product (°C) are analyzed in a matrix diagram. An upward arrow beside the parameters at the start of the rows indicates an increase in the value of the controlling parameters of the process. Similarly, upward and downward arrows in the production output indicate an increase or a decrease in output parameters. Table 6.6 illustrates the input and output parameters and their interdependence in milk powder production process.

**TABLE 6.6**

Controlling parameters of spray-drying

| Parameters | Values | Particle Size | Moisture % | Qty. Output | Qty. Fines | Output Temp. |
|---|---|---|---|---|---|---|
| % water in milk | ↑ | ↓ | ↑ | ↓ | ↑ | |
| Milk temperature | ↑ | | ↓ | ↑ | | |
| Milk density | ↑ | ↑ | ↓ | ↑ | ↓ | |
| Milk viscosity | ↑ | ↑ | | | ↓ | |
| Pump pressure | ↑ | ↓ | ↑ | ↑ | ↑ | |
| Nozzle diameter | ↑ | ↑ | ↑ | ↑ | ↓ | |
| Nozzle separation | ↑ | ↓ | | | | |
| Number of nozzles | ↑ | | ↑ | ↑ | | ↓ |
| Inlet air temperature | ↑ | | ↓ | ↑ | | |
| Exhaust air temperature | ↑ | | ↓ | | | ↑ |
| Inlet air quantity | ↑ | | ↓ | ↑ | ↑ | |

### *Review Questions*

1. Discuss and elaborate on the important guidelines for a successful sampling.
2. What are the twin challenges a problem-solver faces while sampling for investigation.
3. Explain in brief the process for capturing the voice of customers.
4. Explain using examples how the voice of customers can lead us to an actionable point for problem-solving.
5. What are the features of a checklist? How would you arrive at an optimum design for a checklist?
6. Explain the construction of a matrix diagram and its benefits as an important tool for collecting data and collating information.

## References

1. Snedecor, W. George and Cochran, William, G. *Statistical Methods*. New Delhi: Oxford & IBH Publishing, 1967.
2. Pande, Pete, and Holpp, Larry. *What Is Six Sigma?* New York: McGraw-Hill, 2002.
3. Ganapathy, K., Narayana, V., and Subramaniam, B. *New Seven Tools*. Secunderabad: Quality Council Forum of India, 1997.

WHEN GOWRIE MET KRISHNA:

*Gowrie:* Do you think that every problem has a solution?
*Krishna:* Yeah! Something is like this. Mathematics taught me preciously that.

# 7

## Techniques and Tools for Systematic Analysis

Far more critical than what we know or we do not know is what we do not want to know.

**Eric Hoffer**

## Objectives

After going through this chapter and understanding the issues described in it, you will be able to deal more efficiently with the challenges in problem-solving:

1. *Master* the techniques of prioritization.
2. *Learn* the fundamentals of root cause analysis.
3. *Draw* histograms, scatter plots, and run charts.
4. *Develop* Pareto diagrams.
5. *Conduct* systematic data analysis.
6. *Link* the results of potential analysis to potential solutions.

## Chapter at a Glance

In this chapter, we will discuss various techniques and tools for systematic analysis. We will discuss about the simple techniques of prioritization that helps us plan and do things with the available resources in a much better way. We will learn the fundamentals of root cause analysis, and see how Pareto diagrams give us the important and quick information in a nutshell. In order to analyze the data recorded, we will learn the concepts of creating the histograms, scatter plots. We will also learn the process of preparing run charts to follow up the results of the changes or the actions that are taken in the course of problem-solving.

## Techniques for Systematic Analysis

### Prioritization Matrix

Prioritization essentially means to arrange various items that require attention or action in order of their relative importance from highest to lowest. This is to decide what to do and what not to do. To determine what to do first and what to do last. To evaluate what is important and what is not. The process of prioritization becomes important as it is all about selecting a few important and urgent items from a group of tasks in order to derive the most or the optimum value with the least effort. This helps us obtain the highest return from limited resources [1].

There are two aspects of every decision-making process—that which is qualitative and that which is quantitative. Sometimes, prioritization may vary depending on the situation. Consider a striker in a soccer team who is injured during a playoff. While treating the player's injury, the team doctor may only use a muscle sprain spray that will temporarily kill the pain so that the striker can play again instead of taking him out of the stadium and treating him in a clinic.

On the other hand, imagine a student is due to take an examination in the next thirty days. In the meantime, she catches a viral fever and becomes bedridden. As per the doctor and his diagnosis, she must be on full bed rest and avoid any physical and mental stress to achieve a quick and easy recovery. In this case, the student has two options—to continue with some studying and thereby some stress over the coming days and delay the quick recovery process or to fully rest and restart a study regime only after fully recovering. In the latter case, although it is very important to prepare for the examination, the student's priority may be to get well first. Therefore, the student may prioritize and make the decision to fully rest and recover first.

While making decisions on prioritization in problem-solving, we face similar decision-making challenges regarding optimizing importance, effectiveness, and resources available. We follow a systematic approach to assign weights to various parameters in a tabular form and arrive at a common ground. Here, we will learn a few quick techniques consider in the prioritization process.

1. As a first step, the empowered team gathers and discusses the priorities of various activities. These priorities are *must* be done, *should* be done, *could* be done, and *would* be done. Obviously, the *must* be done activities carry the most priority.

   Before starting the prioritization activity, it is important to know the criterion for segregating the available options in line with the aforementioned key words—such as must, should, could, and would.

   i. Must—Safety issues, legal and regulatory compliance issues, potential complaints

ii. Should—Employee welfare, labor welfare, customer delight over customer satisfaction

iii. Could—Compatible to the capability of the present team's skill and resources available

iv. Would—Meant for betterment when the existing works are not good enough

2. Next, we consider the priority quadrant. Here, all the alternatives are assigned various numbers for the quantity of relative value achieved with reference to the amount of effort used. These *value* numbers are plotted as a function of *efforts*. In Figure 7.1, the schematic two-by-two matrix explains the four quadrants of comparative risk versus return. Depending on the situation, one has to prioritize the actions. If the returns are high, one may think of embracing the same. Then one must settle for the option at Quadrants 1 and 2.

3. Next, we visualize priority with distant successive numbers. While a team is critically thinking and weighing the various options available, they may give some rating on a scale of one to ten depending on various aspects such as importance, effectiveness, and so on. Sometimes the issue of central tendency prevails, and team members assign numbers close to five for all the options. This results in not very different final numbers and makes it difficult to evaluate the comparative weight. Therefore, the final decisions may not come from a strong ground. On the other hand, if we assign the numbers in such that that they are very distant, the resulting final number will be very distinct and easier to recognize for decision-making. Instead of numbers on scale of 1 to 10, consider numbers such as 1, 3, 5, 7, and 10. The difference in the consecutive numbers increases as the

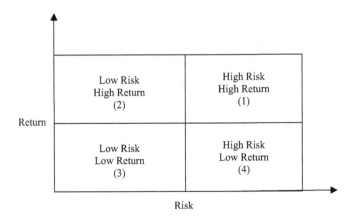

**FIGURE 7.1**
How to prioritize? Return versus risk matrix.

numbers progress higher. This helps in arriving at clearly distinctive decision-making points. By assigning these numbers to the increasing priorities, the team will be better off when making a decision.

When conducting a prioritizing exercise, we must remember that this is essentially a depiction of various parameters in a tabular form, and a corresponding weight should be marked beside the individual parameters. This kind of weight can refer to risks associated with the end product or for the customer, to the probability of the occurrence of a defect, to the importance of various options available, or to probabilities associated with risks. A brainstorming session can be conducted to identify and assign the weights for analysis.

When discussing prioritization and decision-making, it is important to remember a few rules of thumb that are to be followed. The leader as well as the team members should be very methodical in arriving at collaborative solutions. In order to understand these rules of thumb better, the following is a list of a few of those guiding principles.

1. As a leader, be collaborative and be tactical in getting to the point.
2. Ask the relevant questions to the appropriate and relevant people.
3. Look at the whole problem together, instead of only part of it.
4. Strictly avoid prioritization when there is lack of evidence.
5. Try to find out whether the issue under discussion has some other related secondary issues that may affect the character of the primary issue.
6. Avoid using preconceived, biased, or half-hearted solutions to prioritize probable options.
7. Write down all discussion points for a visual review, such as on Post-its® or on whiteboard.

## Real Problem-Solving

### Royal Hartford Prioritizes Action Plan of Customer Feedback

At the Royal Hartford Metals Section Company, the plant manager receives much feedback and many customer complaints. Based on the feedback and complaints, the team leader decides to perform a systematic analysis for mitigating those issues. In the first analysis, it is understood that they need to make some immediate changes in the present ongoing work flow and process in order to address the complaints received. They consider the single factor that most customers mention and try to determine its importance and impact on the overall operational parameters of the company. However, all the problems cannot

**TABLE 7.1**

Various concerns associated with a customer complaint

| | Concerns Associated with Complaint | | | | | | | | |
|---|---|---|---|---|---|---|---|---|---|
| | | | | | Priority No. | | | | |
| Sl | Fixed rubber pad comes out easily, leading to leakage | Imp. | 1 | 2 | 3 | 4 | 5 | I × P |
| 1 | Is this a historical problem? | 20 | √ | | | | | 20 |
| 2 | What is its impact on productivity? | 100 | | √ | | | | 200 |
| 3 | What is its impact on product's overall quality? | 80 | | √ | | | | 160 |
| 4 | What is its impact on OTIF[1] delivery to customer? | 100 | | | | √ | | 400 |
| 5 | What kind of challenges are faced? | 40 | | | | √ | | 160 |
| 6 | How urgent is problem? | 80 | | | | | √ | 400 |
| 7 | What is its impact on profitability? | 40 | | | | | √ | 200 |
| 8 | What are degree of risks associated with it? | 20 | | √ | | | | 40 |

be addressed at once due to lack of time, money, and other related resources. Therefore, the team needs to prioritize and decide for which problem further analysis and corrective actions must be first initiated. For every complaint received, they design a priority table such as that displayed in Table 7.1. Each table is dedicated to one complaint and all the related concerns are listed beside one another, as detailed in the table. The team conducts a brainstorming session, assigns an importance number (how important the complaint is to resolve), and systematically assigns a suitable priority number from one to five to all the concerns. At the column on the far right side of the table, a compound number is calculated by multiplying the priority number by the importance number, and that is noted for further scrutiny.

A careful look at the list derived from the customers' feedback shows that there are concerns that are applicable to all types of customer complaints. These are generic concerns that run the whole gamut of requirements. In the importance column (Imp.), you will find numbers from 20 to 100 that reflect the relative importance of the eight issues listed there. These importance numbers may vary for different complains. Note that the complaint mentioned in the table (fixed rubber pad comes out easily, leading to leakage) has a high impact on productivity (assigned 100), although it is assigned a low priority number (two). On the other hand,

---

[1] OTIF is the abbreviation for "On Time in Full." This refers to supplying the customer with the entire order quantity in full within the scheduled time frame that was mutually agreed upon.

its impact on profitability is not high; but it has a high priority number for taking action. However, its impact on OTIF as well as its priority for initiating action are both very high. On a further careful look at the table, you will find that this complaint's impact on the OTIF delivery to the customer, its impact on productivity, and its impact on profitability are all high. Therefore, the team has to decide on some immediate actions.

This kind of prioritization helps a team decide on a course of action. While conducting such a prioritization exercise, you need to be impartial enough not to become obsessed with one particular issue or to become prejudiced.

### Real Problem-Solving

**Engine Care Department Prioritizes Action Plan of Improvement**

In a mechanical engineering workshop, various types of gears are produced that cater to a diversified market requirement. The engineers on the shop floor experience several problems on a daily basis affecting the production yield. The team identifies a set of problems that they want to address. However, it is well understood that the problems are unique in nature and will require different approaches. A task force is assigned to analyze the situation and asked to find an immediate solution. However, due to limited resources, they decide to prioritize how they will take action. The team then identifies various attributes of the issues and lists their impact using a rating scale of one through ten; the whole exercise is detailed in Table 7.2.

The team collects all the pending issues concerning the engine care division and assigns various attributes based on their impact on quality, productivity, delivery delays, cost of rejection, and customer satisfaction. All the team members discuss these points and give each a rating on a scale of one to ten. All the ratings for a particular issue are added up and total ratings are detailed in the column headed *total*. Based on the rating, the team decides to initiate an immediate action plan for *bad finishing, requiring rework in cylindrical core.*

From the examples cited here, you should have a clear idea how prioritization takes place in an industrial setup. For further practice in this process, look for such situations where you are required to prioritize among various options and initiate suitable actions.

**TABLE 7.2**

Detailed prioritization exercise for pending issues in engine care department

| Pending Issues in Engine Care and Manufacturing | Quality Issues | Productivity Constraints | Delivery Delays | Cost of Rejection | Customer Satisfaction Index | Total |
|---|---|---|---|---|---|---|
| 1. Core drill gets damaged due to wrong entry of shaft | 5 | 8 | 7 | 9 | 5 | 34 |
| 2. Taper angle mismatch in cast pieces, soft drill | 6 | 9 | 6 | 5 | 5 | 31 |
| 3. Tool falling problem | 6 | 8 | 7 | 5 | 7 | 33 |
| 4. Bad finishing, requiring rework in cylindrical core | 7 | 6 | 7 | 8 | 7 | 35 |
| 5. Position shift of core drill due to round ball operation | 6 | 6 | 5 | 6 | 8 | 31 |

7 QUALITY CONTROL TOOLS

---

**Real Problem-Solving**

## Asiatic Faucets Uses Why-Why Analysis to Find the Root Cause

At Asiatic Faucets, Inc., high-end brass and other metal faucets are produced for institutional as well as retail customers worldwide. The process systems have been standardized over many years of operation. The company brings in various new products every year. In the field of faucet manufacturing, Asiatic Faucets commands respect in consumers' minds and is geared up for a great future.

Of late, the molding rejection rate during production of the faucets has been as high as 10%, which calls for re-melting of the brass metal and, as a consequence, a loss in resources and revenue. The team responsible for solving this problem conducts brainstorming sessions and short-lists 21 probable reasons for the high rejection of cast pieces. Then the team runs a prioritizing session and selects the three most important probable reasons that may constitute a contribution to the rejection rate of as much as 95%. These three reasons are listed in Table 7.3.

**TABLE 7.3**

Sorted reasons for high rejection in Asiatic Faucets

| Reasons Sorted as per Importance | | Date: 07/10/2017 |
|---|---|---|
| Problem statement: To reduce molding rejection of Asiatic Faucets from 10% to 4% | | |
| Weighted by Importance: | | # Ranking |
| Item # | Process Input | Most Important |
| 3 | Molding time variation | 300 |
| 7 | Fast de-molding or releasing with respect to SOP | 300 |
| 18 | Smelter is not following SOP | 300 |

*Note:* SOP = standard operating procedure

## Root Cause Analysis

In the previous sections, we have seen that at every stage, the entire problem-solving journey revolves around implementing suitable actions to counter the root cause that created the problem. Therefore, analyzing the problem situation to find out the root cause will remain the most important aspect. Success in problem-solving will depend entirely on success in identifying the root cause. In this section, we will consider the most important technique for root cause analysis, the why–why analysis (Figure 7.2), and discuss it in detail [2].

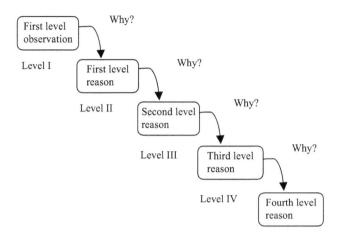

**FIGURE 7.2**
A simple why-why analysis scheme.

The idea is to ask a few "whys" successively. By asking this at every step, we will find some answers. As we proceed, we also will get answers to a few successive "whys." Every answer may require some action.

In Figure 7.3, a problem of delay in product delivery is analyzed using this technique. If you go through the questions and answers, you will find that every answer is questioned till a point where a concrete action might be initiated. Surprisingly, the root cause of the delay in supply is finally determined to be a failure in communication with the customer. Had the customer been informed earlier, the delivery schedule could have been changed to one that was more feasible. The rescheduled delivery date could have been easily met!

After the team sorts out the major contributors, they run a why-why analysis for every short-listed probable reason to understand the root cause and to determine the most suitable action to take. In Table 7.4, we find the outcome of this exercise. The team takes the first reason from Table 7.3 (process input) and asks *why*. They note the *answer*; in some cases, there may be multiple probable answers. After the answers are noted and there is satisfactory deliberation, at the next stage, the same answers are questioned again to get a different set of answers. This process of questioning continues till the team arrives at a workable solution to the question: *Why are the pilot sample cast rate data not available on time?* At this point, the team writes the action to be undertaken: *When pilot melt sample is cast, the team leader should transmit the data to the smelter immediately.* Finally, the plan determined is: (1) The team leader's work shift should be changed to start at the same time as that of the smelter, and (2) the communication board should have the data available for immediate reference.

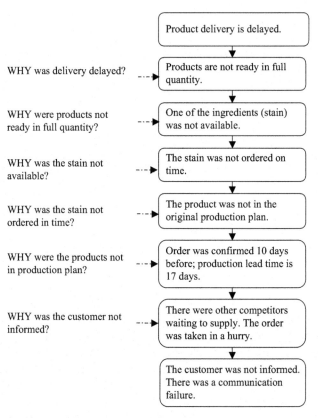

**FIGURE 7.3**
An illustration of why-why analysis for a problem of delay in supply.

## Tools for Systematic Analysis

### Pareto Analysis

Pareto analysis is essentially a tool that brings out the most important from the least important in a set of data in order to differentiate the vital few from the trivial many.

After a required set of data is obtained from the data-gathering check sheets and later is organized to some extent through various techniques and tools, one will be left with many defects to solve, many issues to address, or even many parameters to control.

In this scenario, it will be very difficult to determine where one must focus. For this situation, prioritization will help reduce the problem posed by multiple options. For example, a quality defect may have several causes; however, this does not mean that all the causes have equal significance. There will

**TABLE 7.4**

Why-Why analysis to follow through answers and to determine actions

| | Sr. No | Why | Answer | Action |
|---|---|---|---|---|
| | 1 | Why is there variation in molding time? | 1A. Poor coordination between team leader and smelter. | |
| | | | 1B. Absorption coefficient of pilot cast sample is different on different days. | |
| Why-Why Analysis | 2A | Why is there poor coordination between team leader and smelter? | 2A. Team leader is not available during decision-making time period (the right melting and casting time). | |
| | | | 2B. Pilot sample cast rate data are not available on time. | |
| | 2B | Why is absorption coefficient of pilot cast sample different on different days? | 3A. Variation in melt time and working temperature. | |
| | 2C | Why is team leader not available during decision-making time? | 4A. Work shift of team leader starts at a different time than the smelter. | |
| | 2D | Why are pilot sample cast rate data not available on time? | 5A. Prioritization of work is not done correctly. The team leader is busy doing other important work. | When pilot melt sample is cast, team leader should transmit data to smelter immediately. |
| Exact action planned | 1 | The work shift of the team leader will be changed to start at the same time as that of the smelter. | | |
| | 2 | The communication board will have the data available for immediate reference. | | |

always be some causes that have a large effect on the problem outcome and others that will not have a significant bearing on the outcome. Thus, a set of many possible causes can be divided into two subgroups. The first is those that have a comparatively large effect on the outcome. These are usually lower in number and are called the *vital few*. The other subgroup are those causes that have less of an effect on the outcome. These usually are greater in number and are called the *trivial many*. Research has shown that for a vital few, 20% of variables control 80% of the outcome; the remaining 80% of variables control (the trivial many) control 20% of the outcome. Therefore, the priority will be to identify those 20% (the vital few) and organize the entire problem-solving journey around them. This will not only save energy but also will save time in getting early results and staying motivated for a long problem-solving journey.

Vilfredo Pareto (1848–1923) was an Italian-American socioeconomic researcher who discovered that 80% of a country's wealth is in the hands of 20% of its people. It was later revealed that the mysterious 80/20 ratio, also called the Pareto distribution, is actually prevalent in many other walks of life. For example, the Pareto distribution may be found in several different areas relevant to entrepreneurs and business managers. For example:

1. 80% of a company's revenue comes from 20% of its goods
2. 80% of a company's profits come from 20% of its customers
3. 80% of a company's complaints come from 20% of its customers
4. 80% of a company's profits come from 20% of the time spent by its staff
5. 80% of a company's sales are made by 20% of its sales staff
6. 80% of problems can be attributed to 20% of causes

A Pareto chart may be used in many situations. A few are listed here for a better understanding of the concept:

- When the "vital few" issues are to be segregated from the "trivial many" issues, in order to focus on the most important ones.
- When it is necessary to show a relative change in an addressed issue in comparison to other measured ones.
- When it is important to show that there is a change after improvement takes place in a process.
- It can be used in place of just a bar chart because it contains comparatively more information, especially information on priority.

While using a Pareto diagram, the general tendency is to capture the causes that are vital and to discard the trivial. However, as promulgated by Kaoru Ishikawa, the great Japanese professor and creator of the Ishikawa diagram, sometimes important but less prominent causes, or even problems, are not picked. Therefore, some very important opportunities are lost. Also, the established process might not be equipped to capture these problems within their proper perspectives. An executive engaged in problem-solving must also keep an eye on these aspects too.

The Pareto chart is a bar chart where the bars represent the defects, or various problems, from different sources. The bars are arranged in descending order of their occurrence or importance. A line graph of the cumulative number of defectives is also drawn in the same chart on the secondary axis. Usually the defect entities are on the X-axis and the number of defects is on the left Y-axis. The cumulative percentage of defects curve is drawn on the right Y-axis.

## Practical Pareto Analysis in Action

The producer of a certain industrially manufactured product has received several customer complaints. After the complaints are tabulated and organized in a descending order, the set of data evolved is noted as in Table 7.5.

In Table 7.5, Column C refers to the number of defects, and Column D refers to the percent of defects with reference to the total defects. A careful look at the table shows that out of all the 15 defects, only the first 3 defects (precisely 20%!) yielded a cumulative percentage of 80.9% (Column E). The first 3 defects are the *vital few* and the remaining 12 defects are the *trivial many*. The resulting Pareto chart may look like the one in Figure 7.4.

This analysis provides a problem-solving strategy direction in which we should focus our attention for these vital few causes to get maximum results.

**TABLE 7.5**

Various defects observed in a vitreous china whiteware product

| A | B | C | D | E |
|---|---|---|---|---|
| Sl No | Causes | #Defects | %Defect | Cumulative% |
| 1 | Bloating | 76 | 43.93 | 43.9% |
| 2 | Ramp Crack | 50 | 28.90 | 72.8% |
| 3 | Foot Crack | 14 | 8.09 | 80.9% |
| 4 | Edge Stress | 5 | 2.89 | 83.8% |
| 5 | Specks | 4 | 2.31 | 86.1% |
| 6 | Web Crack | 4 | 2.31 | 88.4% |
| 7 | Spangling | 4 | 2.31 | 90.8% |
| 8 | Body Dirt | 3 | 1.73 | 92.5% |
| 9 | Run Down | 3 | 1.73 | 94.2% |
| 10 | Col Variation | 2 | 1.16 | 95.4% |
| 11 | Sagging | 2 | 1.16 | 96.5% |
| 12 | Logo Fault | 2 | 1.16 | 97.7% |
| 13 | Scratch | 2 | 1.16 | 98.8% |
| 14 | Undulation | 1 | 0.58 | 99.4% |
| 15 | Edge Crawling | 1 | 0.58 | 100.0% |
| | Total | 173 | | |

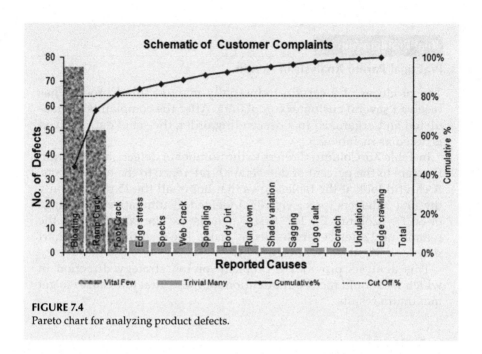

**FIGURE 7.4**
Pareto chart for analyzing product defects.

WHY-WHY

## Histograms

Let us refer to the discussions in the previous chapters. After the data are collected in the standardized format of a check sheet, one needs to look for any pattern or trend in the data set. A quick tool to use may be a histogram. A histogram is a graphical representation of frequency distribution for a set of data (usually depicted either with horizontal or vertical bars), which may display variations in a process. Histograms also show dispersion and shape (relative frequency) of data; they are used to check where the greatest variations occur in a process. They may also give some indication whether the process specifications are exceeded anywhere. They help us understand that a process is capable of meeting its specifications.

A histogram can be used to determine whether process variation is normal or if there is something in the process that has caused the output to be produced in an unusual way. A histogram can be created by following a few simple steps:

- Count the number of data points collected in the data set.
- Identify the range of the entire data set (R).
- Define some equal intervals—called the class width (H)—so that H = R/K; K is the number of classes.
- Determine the end values.
- Construct a frequency table based on the values determined in the previous steps.
- Construct a histogram from the frequency table.

### Real Problem-Solving

### How Does the Length of the Cane Sticks Vary in the Pack?

In order to understand the application of histograms, let us use an example. The sample data of the length of 50 cane sticks ordered by a customer is detailed in Table 7.6. The customer informs us that there is a variation in the lengths of the cane sticks. You want to analyze and understand the extent of this variation. A histogram will help you.

The data listed in Table 7.6 are all independent and are expressed in a tabular format in order to assign an address to every data, such as A1 (699), E6 (675), and so on. This set of 50 measurements does not really provide us with any trend for the lengths of the cane sticks. No specific conclusion may be made from this information. Therefore, to analyze the data distribution, we need to group the data in a defined fashion. After an initial look at the data, we find that the maximum and minimum lengths are 735 mm and 650 mm, respectively. We set

**TABLE 7.6**

Lengths of 50 cane sticks received by a customer

|    | A   | B   | C   | D   | E   |
|----|-----|-----|-----|-----|-----|
| 1  | 699 | 689 | 685 | 667 | 719 |
| 2  | 690 | 700 | 687 | 656 | 724 |
| 3  | 696 | 695 | 706 | 657 | 716 |
| 4  | 685 | 704 | 686 | 689 | 694 |
| 5  | 650 | 712 | 695 | 683 | 719 |
| 6  | 659 | 735 | 694 | 702 | 675 |
| 7  | 672 | 726 | 691 | 695 | 685 |
| 8  | 675 | 713 | 689 | 705 | 710 |
| 9  | 680 | 684 | 658 | 706 | 684 |
| 10 | 686 | 721 | 656 | 695 | 696 |

an imaginary group with a span of 10 mm starting at 651 mm. Here, the value 650 is eliminated from the range data just for simplification. Next, we find how many data points are available in each of the spans.

In Table 7.7, you will find the frequency of data. The graph on the right shows the histogram.

In Table 7.7, note that all the bars have equal width and the height or length of the bars depends on the frequency of occurrence. The fixed width of a histogram is called a cell, a bin, or a class, and is a fixed range of measurements. This graph also tells us that the cane stick lengths follow a particular fashion. Most sizes are in the range of 681 mm to 690 mm. The lowest numbers of cane stick lengths are located at around 661 mm to 670 mm and 731 to 740 mm. Thus, the histogram gives us a quick visual summary of the entire data set.

**TABLE 7.7**

Frequency table and histogram for the cane length data set

| Range | | | |
|-------|-------|------|---|
| **Min** | **Max** | **Freq** | |
| 661 | 670 | 1 | |
| 671 | 680 | 4 | |
| 681 | 690 | 13 | |
| 691 | 700 | 11 | |
| 701 | 710 | 6 | |
| 711 | 720 | 5 | |
| 721 | 730 | 3 | |
| 731 | 740 | 1 | |

In an industrial situation, knowing how to correctly read histogram data will help one judge the exact nature of the process parameters and thereby further the process of data analysis.

## Patterns of Histograms

Different sets of data can have different types of histograms. Figures 7.5 to 7.15 deal with various types of histograms that we encounter in everyday life. A schematic is provided on the left-hand sides of the figures, and the aspects of the patterns are noted in the adjacent columns. A brief interpretation is also added.

It is worthwhile here to note a few situations where a histogram can be used.

1. When *multiple sets of data have interdependence* and we want to know which one is dependent on what.
2. When it is understood or suspected that there are *multiple factors affecting the process*; when we need to see the dependence in a distribution.
3. When an investigation of actual distribution may help in *defining the upper control limits and lower control limits*.
4. When we need to find out the *tendency of the distribution in order to find further attributes*.

## Stratification

Stratification is essentially a classification of a set of data into categories and subcategories on the basis of some chosen criterion. Usually, in a process setup, there are defects or nonconformities that occur together with various

**FIGURE 7.5**
Histogram with high frequency and a few bars.

Aspect:
Low frequency with a few bars

Interpretation:
Distribution is flat. Some data
points are absent. The process is
not under control.

**FIGURE 7.6**
Histogram with low frequency and a few bars.

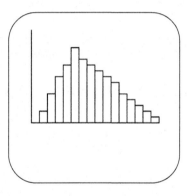

Aspects:
Skewed frequency with a few
bars, wherein the highest
frequency bars are either toward
right (negative) or left (positive).

Interpretation
This may be a natural distribution.
Maybe the data are insufficient or
all the data have not been collected
from the available set.

**FIGURE 7.7**
Histogram with skewed frequency and a few bars.

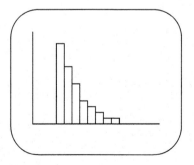

Aspect:
Exponentially distributed

Interpretation:
This is extremely skewed
frequency distribution.

**FIGURE 7.8**
Histogram with skewed frequency and a few bars.

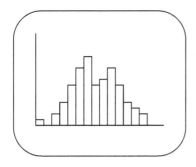

**FIGURE 7.9**
Histogram with extremely skewed frequency and a few bars.

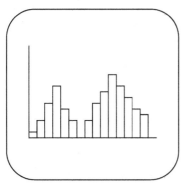

**FIGURE 7.10**
Histogram with two-peak distribution.

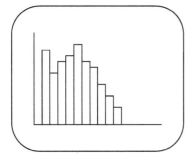

**FIGURE 7.11**
Histogram with edge-peaked bars.

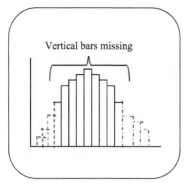

**FIGURE 7.12**
Histogram with bars truncated at end.

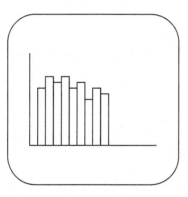

**FIGURE 7.13**
Histogram with plateau or unitary distribution.

**FIGURE 7.14**
Histogram with combed bars.

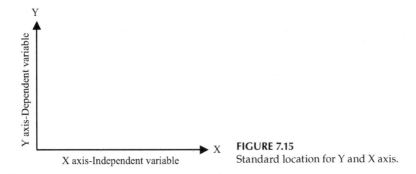

**FIGURE 7.15**
Standard location for Y and X axis.

other entities in the input end of the cause-and-effect diagram. It will be a challenge to find out the exact domain where the causes are really occurring and contributing to the final problem. To find a pattern at this stage, stratification of various data will be necessary. Essentially, this means that in a single strata all the entries in a data set must have common characteristics. The total data set is divided into subsets, and comparisons are made. For instance, imagine that some defects are occurring in an industrially manufactured product where a 24/7 manufacturing process is utilized by a total of around 700 people who are working within that process. Further imagine that the same problem has been occurring for quite a few days and this is not the only time this problem has occurred. It usually resurfaces after a dormant phase of several days or months.

In such cases, data are collected and systematically organized in such a manner that the relationship of the nonconformity can be established in reference to various possible input causal entities, such as raw materials, types of product specifications, different product patterns in the same group of products, working shifts (night, evening, morning, and so on), months of the year (pertaining to particular seasons or conditions, such as rainy, summer, winter, or even sudden changes in temperature and humidity, such as in spring and autumn), workers employed on a particular machine, a specific machine deployed for production, and a particular time of a day. This type of data organization using segmented elements is called stratification.

Some cautions when using stratification for data analysis are as follows:

- Treating known sources of variability as unknown and stratifying may not yield sensible results.
- Over-stratification to an extreme also may not produce sensible data for understanding the situation.
- Limited stratification may help us to understand the situation better.

## Real Problem-Solving

### Is Cord a Glass Problem?

Imagine that in an industrially manufactured product, a frequent problem of "cord" appears as often as 6% of the time over the period of the last three days compared to an average of 0.5% in the last six months. This sudden rise requires a quick analysis and immediate action to reduce the defect. The present knowledge indicates that the defect may surface because of a technical nonconformity, a manual mistake (in raw material batch mixing), or even the wrong selection of raw materials. In a continuous production line, the defective products also are sorted (before packing) in three different production lines. This shows that though the initial batching starts in the same place, the in-process products eventually are distributed in different production lines; therefore, different sets of people contribute manually before the final product is made.

In order to determine the exact nature of the defect and its arrival frequency, we need to understand the trend of how the defect or problem is distributed with reference to the production shifts, the booth where the electrical circuit was coated, the coating operator, the production line, and so on. After a Pareto analysis is conducted, a group of workmen was selected for further study. It was found that on an average, the defect occurred more often with respect to products impacted by these workmen. The results are summarized in Table 7.8. The operator details are recorded in the first column, and the observed defect percentages are recorded in the other columns for six days of operation.

If we analyze this table, we find that over a period of six days, there is a clear trend indicating that Operator #796 is generating fewer defects on average. However, for the other two operators, the defects are on the higher side. There is no clear trend of more defects being generated by any particular workman.

The base data set for approximately five days is stratified again irrespective of operators to see whether there is any trend in defect appearance with reference to the shifts in which the defects were produced.

**TABLE 7.8**

Percentage of defects observed for operators in a span of six days

| Workmen #/Dates | Day 1 | Day 2 | Day 3 | Day 4 | Day 5 | Day 6 | Average |
|---|---|---|---|---|---|---|---|
| #796 | 4.95 | 2.31 | 3.67 | 2.98 | 3.1 | 4.32 | 3.56 |
| #403 | 6.78 | 3.87 | 2.98 | 1.63 | 4.32 | 6.27 | 4.31 |
| #118 | 2.56 | 5.65 | 4.89 | 3.65 | 6.32 | 5.68 | 4.79 |
| Average% | 4.76 | 3.94 | 3.85 | 2.75 | 4.58 | 5.42 | 4.22 |

**TABLE 7.9**

Occurrence of defects in different shifts

| Shifts   Time | Dates | | | | | Min | Max | Average% |
|---|---|---|---|---|---|---|---|---|
| | Day 1 | Day 2 | Day 3 | Day 4 | Day 5 | | | |
| A (07–15 hrs) | 6.78 | 2.32 | 4.56 | 3.54 | 3.65 | 2.32 | 6.78 | 4.30 |
| B (15–23 hrs) | 5.87 | 3.42 | 5.82 | 7.21 | 4.56 | 3.42 | 7.21 | 5.38 |
| C (23–07 hrs) | 2.98 | 7.38 | 4.76 | 3.98 | 7.23 | 2.98 | 7.38 | 5.27 |
| Average% | 5.21 | 4.37 | 5.05 | 4.91 | 5.90 | 4.37 | 5.90 | |

Table 7.9 shows that the minimum and maximum defects vary in a wide range on different days. There is no indication that the defects occur in a greater quantity during any of the specific shifts. Therefore, at this stage, it might be safely concluded that the problem originated somewhere else. Similarly, a data set may be organized to find the correlation between other input entities and the defects.

## Scatter Diagram

A scatter diagram (also known as a scatter plot and an X–Y plot) is a graphical representation of two variables for observing relationships between pairs of variables, wherein the changes in one variable is followed through in the changes in another variable. Usually, two variables are plotted on an X–Y graph sheet. The two variables are not considered to have a cause and effect relationship, although that is suspected. It is only thought that both the variables may occur together. A possibility arises that perhaps both the variables originated from the same cause, and that there may be a secondary correlation between the two variables. If the variables are correlated, then the resulting trend line from the data points will form a straight line or a curve. As the degree of correlation increases, the points become better aligned for a close-knit straight line or a curve. In this case, if we see a clear correlation and do not see a cloud of data points on the graph sheet, we will start to understand the straight-line function $Y = m(X) + C$. However, the problem-solving team must keep in mind that a relationship in the scatter plot might be coincidental, and there may be some other real cause that is responsible for the pseudo-dependence of the parameters in question.

Imagine an inorganic glass composition is being melted in a glass tank furnace. As the melting process reaches maturity, the glass becomes more and more transparent. During this time, the glass defects also are drastically reduced. Therefore, if a plot is drawn between the defect density and the transparency of the resultant glass melt, there will be a positive correlation between the two because both variables are positively correlated to the

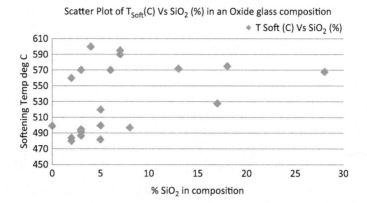

**FIGURE 7.16**
Scatter plot T Soft vs % $SiO_2$.

temperature of the furnace. While a cause-effect relationship is not expected to exist, any one of the variables may be plotted in the horizontal X-axis. However, if the variables are known to have some correlation, it would be advisable to have the independent variable in the X-axis. The general notion for axis selection is depicted in Figure 7.16.

In the event that one variable is suspected to have some bearing on the other, the X–Y plot definitely will show a direct correlation. However, care must be taken while plotting the correlation curve that both the variables can be measured together while all other conditions remain constant (or unchanged as much as possible); otherwise, in all probability, the plots may not show the actual correlation.

Therefore, though a scatter diagram is not sufficient to prove a cause and effect relationship, it may be used to gather necessary evidence for the same. A clear understanding of a process/production/service system will further help establish a cause-and-effect relationship and the creation of a related hypothesis. A scatter diagram/plot can be used for numerous situations, such as the following:

a. To study the possible relationship between one variable and another
b. To measure/understand a process during problem definition
c. To identify a possible causal relationship and root causes
d. To determine whether two effects that appear simultaneously and seem to be related result from the same cause
e. To check the final solution for change and improvements as to whether the implemented changed parameters have a positive correlation to the results obtained

## How Mineral Oxides Affect the Properties of Inorganic Glass?

In the Shanghai Blue Parrot Glass Company, various oxide glasses are produced. In one such inorganic glass composition, there are six different oxides. The compositions of the oxides are noted in Columns 1 to 6 of Table 7.10. In Rows 1 to 21, various oxides' contents (as a percentage) are provided for the glass sample compositions. The oxide contents total 100% in all the cases.

**TABLE 7.10**

Oxide composition of various inorganic glasses

| | Glass Composition | | | | | | Properties | |
|---|---|---|---|---|---|---|---|---|
| Sample # | %SiO$_2$ | %Al$_2$O$_3$ | %B$_2$O$_3$ | %BaO | %ZnO | %PbO | CTE (%/C) | T$_{Soft}$ (C) |
| | Col 1 | Col 2 | Col 3 | Col 4 | Col 5 | Col 6 | Col 7 | Col 8 |
| 1 | 3 | 0 | 21 | 0 | 21 | 55 | 77 | 492 |
| 2 | 0 | 0 | 28 | 0 | 10 | 62 | 78 | 499 |
| 3 | 5 | 0 | 19 | 0 | 20 | 56 | 74 | 500 |
| 4 | 3 | 4 | 17 | 0 | 20 | 56 | 74 | 487 |
| 5 | 3 | 0 | 21 | 0 | 23 | 53 | 73 | 495 |
| 6 | 2 | 4 | 22 | 0 | 10 | 62 | 80 | 484 |
| 7 | 2 | 8 | 19 | 0 | 8 | 63 | 80 | 480 |
| 8 | 5 | 8 | 19 | 0 | 6 | 62 | 76 | 500 |
| 9 | 8 | 0 | 15 | 0 | 21 | 56 | 75 | 497 |
| 10 | 5 | 0 | 15 | 0 | 24 | 56 | 75 | 482 |
| 11 | 5 | 0 | 22 | 0 | 23 | 50 | 71 | 520 |
| 12 | 7 | 0 | 22 | 28 | 33 | 10 | 77 | 595 |
| 13 | 4 | 0 | 30 | 28 | 28 | 10 | 77 | 600 |
| 14 | 7 | 0 | 24 | 23 | 26 | 20 | 75 | 590 |
| 15 | 6 | 0 | 22 | 18 | 21 | 33 | 75 | 570 |
| 16 | 28 | 1 | 5 | 0 | 1 | 65 | 69 | 568 |
| 17 | 18 | 4 | 16 | 10 | 2 | 50 | 73 | 575 |
| 18 | 13 | 6 | 22 | 12 | 2 | 45 | 75 | 572 |
| 19 | 17 | 5 | 2 | 0 | 5 | 71 | 73 | 528 |
| 20 | 3 | 0 | 38 | 28 | 0 | 31 | 82 | 570 |
| 21 | 2 | 0 | 37 | 21 | 0 | 40 | 75 | 560 |

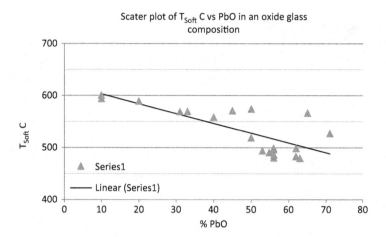

**FIGURE 7.17**
Scatter plot of $T_{Soft}$ C vs PbO in an oxide glass composition.

The glass properties, such as the coefficient of thermal expansion (CTE) and softening temperature ($T_{Soft}$), depend on the constituent oxides. Columns 7 and 8 in Table 7.10 provide these properties for all the 21 glass compositions. In order to ascertain the dependence of these properties on the constituent oxides, a scatter plot can be drawn. To test the dependence, a $T_{Soft}$ versus % silicon dioxide ($SiO_2$) scatter plot is drawn, as in Figure 7.17.

From this plot, it is evident that in the lower addition level of $SiO_2$, the softening temperature does not have a significant trend (dependence) on the quantity of $SiO_2$. However, for different glasses, the softening temperature is different for little variations in $SiO_2$ in the composition range until 10%. For comparatively higher addition levels, from 15% to 30%, the graph is linear; so, there still is no remarkable dependence in this range of $SiO_2$.

In the scatter plot of $T_{Soft}$ versus the percentage of PbO, in Figure 7.18, there is a clear trend line, which shows that upon addition of a percentage of PbO

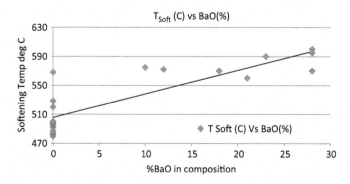

**FIGURE 7.18**
Scatter plot of $T_{Soft}$ C vs BaO in an oxide glass composition.

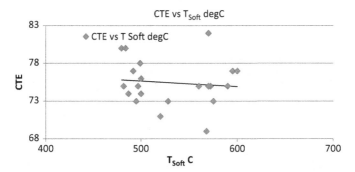

**FIGURE 7.19**
Scatter plot of CTE vs Softening Temperature C in an oxide glass composition.

in the glass composition, the softening temperature reduces significantly. Therefore, $T_{Soft}$ depends on the percentage of PbO. Similarly, in Figure 7.18, the scatter plot of $T_{Soft}$ C versus the percentage of barium oxide (BaO) shows that the softening temperature of the glass increases with an increase in the percentage of BaO in the glass, which means that there is a positive correlation between these two parameters.

In Figure 7.19, a scatter plot of CTE versus $T_{Soft}$ C, the data points clearly are very scattered; however, there is a trend line that shows that the CTE decreases when the $T_{Soft}$ C increases in the temperature range of 500°C to 600°C.

Because both parameters are the resulting properties of the given set of sample glass under consideration, these two are also interdependent. In the entire plot, if the correlation is reasonably linear, then a correlation coefficient may be calculated. One has to interpret the diagram and act.

### Patterns of Scatter Diagrams

If we consider different kinds of dependence profiles, we observe the various shapes that a scatter plot may assume. The schematic plots shown in Figures 7.20 to 7.27 demonstrate the different types of scatter plots. In the adjacent location in the respective figures, you will find the degree of correlation and the possible interpretations. These schematics will help us to better understand scatter plots in general.

In the previous section, we have discussed various types of scatter plots as well as the purposes, contexts, and processes to which they may be applied. These are visual tools used to establish a cause-and-effect relationship between input and output.

## Control Charts

Control charts are a visual display of the data generated continuously from the operation of the process [3]. These types of control charts are special categories

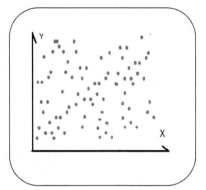

Degree of correlation: None

Interpretation: The data points are uniformly distributed in the plot area. No relationship is evident. The parameter in the vertical Y axis seems to have no dependence on the parameters in the X axis.

**FIGURE 7.20**
Schematic of scatter plot having uniformly distributed data points with no degree of correlation.

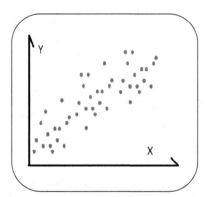

Degree of correlation: Low

Interpretation: Compared to the data distribution in the no- relationship situation, here there lies a faint relationship. The cause in the X axis may have a very distant bearing on the effect. One should find out a more immediate cause to assign to the effect.

**FIGURE 7.21**
Schematic of scatter plot having distributed data points with low degree of correlation.

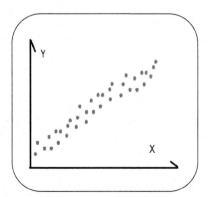

Degree of correlation: High
Interpretation: Here the data points are found to be in a very coherent and closely knit manner; therefore, a trend line is evident. It is highly probable that the effect is highly dependent on the cause. Therefore, it can be assumed that any change in the cause will surely bring an equally reasonable certainty in effect.

**FIGURE 7.22**
Schematic of scatter plot having distributed data points with high degree of correlation.

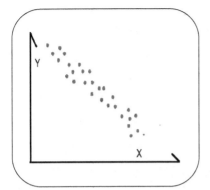

Degree of correlation: Negative

Interpretation: Unlike the plot with a positive correlation, here the effect decreases with the increase in cause.

**FIGURE 7.23**
Schematic of scatter plot having distributed data points with negative degree of correlation.

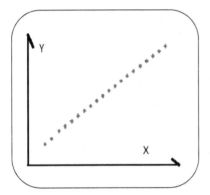

Degree of correlation: Perfect

Interpretation: In this plot, all the data points are in a straight line. This means that the cause has a direct correlation with the effect. Since the resultant plot function is a straight or nearly straight line, it is possible to predict the effect for any change in the cause.

**FIGURE 7.24**
Schematic of scatter plot having distributed data points with perfect degree of correlation.

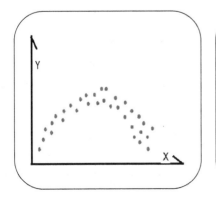

Degree of correlation: Curved

Interpretation: In case of curvilinear output, the type of shape may be of C, U and S and their mirror versions.

**FIGURE 7.25**
Schematic of scatter plot having distributed data points with a curvilinear degree of correlation.

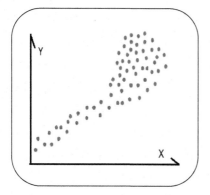

Degree of correlation: Partially linear

Interpretation: A typical plot may have one part that is a straight line and rest fully scattered. The crest data points may indicate the presence of some other parameters, that the initial cause has been discontinued, and other causes are now impacting the data or the cause may have now different parameter.

**FIGURE 7.26**
Schematic of scatter plot having distributed data points with partially linear degree of correlation.

of graphs wherein the process parameters are graphically plotted against time or shifts around the clock. The upper limit and the lower limit of the parameters' specifications are also depicted in the same graph so that the progress of the time-dependent plot can be analyzed continuously with reference to the limits.

These types of charts are used in many situations when it is important:

- To identify and establish a base level of the process performance
- To identify the changes and variations in the process
- To identify the source of variations in the process and the reasons for particular trends
- To identify the presence of special cause variation within process
- To identify when a process has gone out of control
- To identify and compare the historical trends in the process with the present trends after some problem-solving actions have been undertaken

Among many other benefits, a control chart provides important information about process parameters over a period of time.

- It provides diagnostic information so that an operator can understand the status of the process through the pattern of the data. It provides an opportunity to identify the changes required.
- It provides a quick response guide by helping to distinguish between common cause variation (the chance causes) and special cause variations (the assignable causes).
- It provides an opportunity to act in real time after only a short interval, thereby resulting the chance of defects in production. Thus, it helps reduce the process wastes and rework load and improves the productivity and yield.

In order to prepare a control chart, one need to follow a few simple steps, which are outlined briefly here.

- *Determine what is being measured.* For example, a change in body weight with respect to nutrients available in food intake or the number of bubble defects per unit volume of amorphous glass product over a period of time.
- *Determine the period of measurement and the intervals for time increments and time measurements.* For example, the variation in attributes with respect to an eight-hour shift, a day, or several months.
- *Create a simple line graph* by locating the independent variable (the time) on the X-axis (the horizontal axis) and the dependent variable (the measured data) on the Y-axis (the vertical axis).
- *Plot the collected data* as dots on the graph paper and join the dots with a straight line.

The control charts are of two types—Variable charts and Attribute charts. The characteristics of these charts are detailed below:

**Variable charts:**

a. Generally these charts use only one criterion per chart, though there can be multiple variables of the same criterion per chart
b. These charts use measured values, such as, % defects, diameters, cycle time, etc.
c. It might become more expensive as more data collection is required, but they contain more data

**Attribute charts:**

a. There can be multiple characteristics per chart
b. These charts display various attributes such as Go/No Go, Good/Bad, Pass/Fail etc.
c. These are generally less expensive to prepare, but they contain less data

While reviewing the control charts, one may infer information about the progress of the process. Either the process is *In Control* or the process is *Out of Control*. Following criterion will be indicative.

The process is *In Control* if

a. There is no special cause variations present.
b. All variation is random.

The process is *Out of Control* if

a. There is at least one special cause present.
b. Some variation in the chart is random.

Some of the example of Variable control charts are:

a. **X-Bar Chart:** This is a plot of the sample means over time.
b. **R Chart:** This is a plot of the range (difference between highest and lowest values) of a sample over time.
c. **Moving Range Chart:** This is a plot of the moving range over time. A progressive three day average of a sample data can be an example of the same.
d. **Individuals Chart:** This is a plot of the individual values over time.

The averages and ranges are two sensitive kinds of data. These are plotted together to form X-Bar and R charts. This is the most powerful of all control charts to diagnose all production troubles. Next in importance is the p-chart which is an attribute chart.

Some of the example of Attribute control charts are as under:

**p-chart:** p Stands for proportion. These are percentage charts. The p-chart relies more on job knowledge than the X-Bar and R charts. Therefore, it is used mainly where the important causes are known.

**Np-charts:** While plotting p-chart, if the sample sizes are all of same, it is easier to plot the number of defectives found in each sample instead of calculating the percentage. This type of chart is called np-chart, where n is the number of units in a sample. This chart is same as that of p-chart, except for plotting number of defective instead of percentage or fraction.

**c-charts:** The c-chart uses number of 'defects' instead of 'defectives'. Here it is important to understand the difference between the 'defect' and the 'defectives'. A 'defect' is one instance of failure against a single criterion. On the other hand a 'defective' is a unit of product which contains one of more 'defects'. Therefore, it is possible to have one defective unit to contain many defects. A c-chart can be considered as a special form of p-chart. In which a) the possibilities are theoretically infinite and b) the probability of getting a defect at any specific point is infinitesimally small. For a complicated product, the number of defects increases very rapidly. In that case, a c-chart is more appropriate. A few examples where this can be used are:

a. Number of defects in a square meter of surface,
b. Number of points where breakdown occurs per thousand meter of insulated wire,
c. Number of foreign particles in an amber block,
d. Number of failures reported in an airborne early warning system.

c-charts are plotted, marked and interpreted in the same way as that of p-charts.

**u-charts:** This chart is a variation of the c-chart. In this case the average number of defects per unit in a sample of n units are plotted. Each sample of n units will satisfy the requirements of a c-chart. This type of charts are used in aircraft manufacturing, radar systems, and similar multi-variant complicated systems.

In Figure 7.27, a decision making flow chart is presented summarizing the process of selecting an appropriate control charts. In Figure 7.28, for a better understanding of the various types of attribute chart types, a schematic is drawn with reference to lot sizes, defects and defectives.

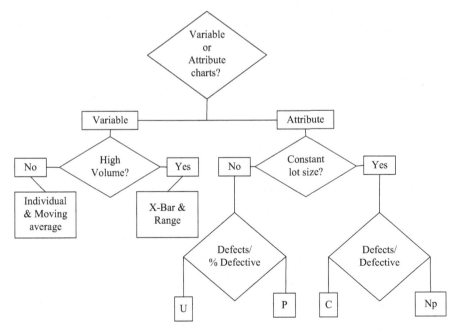

**FIGURE 7.27**
Guideline for selecting an appropriate control chart.

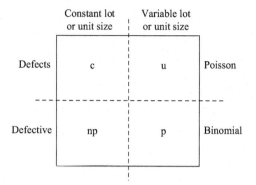

**FIGURE 7.28**
Classification of attribute chart types.

---

**Real Problem-Solving**

### How Does Axis Control the Paint Blisters that Causes Scaling?

In the Axis Metal Sections Company, which is renowned for producing powder-coated metal furniture, there have been frequent observations of paint blisters resulting in scaling and defects in the metal surface. The process control team members have been collecting and collating data from the entire process. After the initial analysis, the team zeroed in on two areas of process variation that are considered to have a positive contribution to the origin of the defects. These are (a) quality of metal surface preparation and (b) variation of temperature in the component drier. The surface preparation department and the drying department have initiated separate actions to control the erratic situation. The engineers in the drying section of the process department have replaced a faulty heater and the PLC[2] to control the temperature. After the change implementations are complete, the temperature of the controlled atmosphere of the drying chamber is recorded over 12 hours for a span of seven days, as detailed in Table 7.11.

The upper control limit and the lower control limit of the process are assigned as 25.5°C and 19.5°C, respectively, as mentioned in the table. In order to understand the behavior of the drier, the temperature profile is plotted in the control chart provided in Figure 7.29. We can then see how the temperature progresses over time and the

---

[2] PLC: Programmable Logic Controllers

**TABLE 7.11**

Variation of temperature in the controlled atmosphere of a reaction chamber

| Time | Day 1 | Day 2 | Day 3 | Day 4 | Day 5 | Day 6 | Day 7 | UCL | LCL |
|---|---|---|---|---|---|---|---|---|---|
| 00 hrs | 21 | 23 | 21 | 21 | 25 | 21 | 23 | 25.5 | 19.5 |
| 01 hrs | 25 | 22 | 20 | 22 | 22 | 20 | 22 | 25.5 | 19.5 |
| 2 hrs | 24 | 21 | 24 | 20 | 24 | 24 | 24 | 25.5 | 19.5 |
| 3 hrs | 24 | 23 | 25 | 22 | 23 | 24 | 24 | 25.5 | 19.5 |
| 4 hrs | 21 | 21 | 21 | 20 | 21 | 20 | 20 | 25.5 | 19.5 |
| 5 hrs | 24 | 24 | 24 | 22 | 22 | 20 | 20 | 25.5 | 19.5 |
| 6 hrs | 21 | 24 | 20 | 21 | 24 | 25 | 21 | 25.5 | 19.5 |
| 7 hrs | 24 | 21 | 20 | 21 | 23 | 24 | 24 | 25.5 | 19.5 |
| 8 hrs | 24 | 23 | 21 | 23 | 24 | 20 | 25 | 25.5 | 19.5 |
| 9 hrs | 24 | 20 | 25 | 21 | 23 | 22 | 25 | 25.5 | 19.5 |
| 10 hrs | 25 | 24 | 21 | 25 | 22 | 22 | 23 | 25.5 | 19.5 |
| 11 hrs | 22 | 25 | 24 | 21 | 24 | 20 | 24 | 25.5 | 19.5 |
| 12 hrs | 22 | 23 | 25 | 23 | 20 | 21 | 22 | 25.5 | 19.5 |

*Note:* UCL: Upper Control Limit
LCL: Lower Control Limit

related variations. For clarity in the schematic, data are plotted for only two days.

This time-dependent schematic tells us the entire process history in one display. If this is followed, one may well understand that the variation in temperature is fluctuating in a cyclical manner. This may give rise to further analysis. This also will help us understand how this variation compares with the variations that occurred before the problem-solving actions were taken. This variation can also be assigned to some common attributable cause.

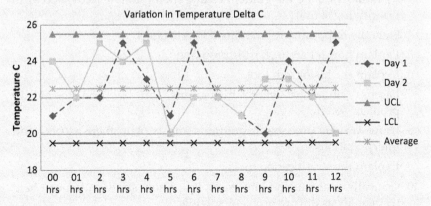

**FIGURE 7.29**
Variation of temperature in the controlled atmosphere of a drying chamber.

PERPETUAL SOLUTION

### Review Questions

1. Explain the fundamental steps in prioritizing the activities for problem-solving.
2. Explain how a risk versus return matrix may help prioritize information during the decision-making process.
3. As a leader of the problem-solving team, while assigning the priority numbers, state the guidelines one should follow for a successful prioritizing activity.
4. State the importance of making a Pareto chart.
5. Explain how a Pareto chart is prepared.
6. Explain the histogram tool.
7. Discuss situations where histograms can be used to aid in problem-solving.
8. Draw various probable histograms and explain their aspects and interpretations.
9. Explain the stratification tool.
10. Critically evaluate and cite examples of how stratification can help us in analysis during problem-solving.
11. Draw various types of scatter diagrams and explain their aspects and interpretation.

12. Explain how a control chart is prepared.

13. Briefly explain the benefits of using a control chart.

14. State when and under what situations control charts can be used.

## References

1. Raju, N. V. S. *Total Quality Management*. New Delhi: Cengage Learning, 2014.
2. Sugiura, T. and Yamada, Y. *The QC Storyline: A Guide to Solving Problems and Communicating the Results*. Tokyo: Asian Productivity Organization, 1995.
3. Western Electric Company Integrated. *Statistical Quality Control Handbook*. New York: Western Electric Company Integrated, 1956.

WHEN GOWRIE MET KRISHNA:

*Gowrie:* My efforts are getting scattered. I am not able to harvest from my efforts! What kind of life am I living?

*Krishna:* You look so perplexed! It is not what you gather but what you scatter that tells what kind of life you have lived.

# 8

## Techniques and Tools for Implementation of Solution and Change Management

Any change, even a change for the better, is always accompanied by drawbacks and discomforts.

**Arnold Bennett**

### Objectives

After going through this chapter and understanding the issues described in it, you will be able to deal more efficiently with the challenges in problem-solving:

1. *Use* the Poka-Yoke technique to prevent reoccurrence of the same problem.
2. *Conduct* a failure mode effect analysis (FMEA) to bring the concepts to a fruitful conclusion.
3. *Describe* the entire problem-solving journey by documenting it in an easily comprehensible manner.
4. *List* all the opinions and counter opinions through a network and stakeholders' analysis.

### Chapter at a Glance

In this chapter we will discuss in detail about various techniques and tools for implementation of solution and the corresponding requirements for change management. We will review the techniques of the famed mistake-proofing technique, Poka-Yoke. We will also discuss various issues related to a successful Failure Mode Effect Analysis. In analyzing the effects of change implementation, we will also try to understand the process for doing stake-holder analysis process and try to draw a network diagram to know the path of a natural process flow. While implementing the desired change, we will also learn about systematic A3 reporting process and facets of a One Point Learning methodology.

## Poka-Yoke

### Mistake-Proofing Strategy

After a problem-solver understands the root cause of a problem and takes the necessary corrective actions, the problem-solver starts to think about how to prevent the occurrence of the same problem again, even by way of a mistake. This refers to the so-called mistake-proofing, the concepts of Poka-Yoke [1]. These concepts are so robust that the preventive action is applicable and effective for any user in a similar situation, anywhere and anytime. The ultimate success of a problem-solver comes from taking appropriate action that prevents future occurrences of the problem. Poka-Yoke, a form of "error-proofing" that makes it impossible for a person to do a job in the wrong way. This is a technique for preventing errors from occurring and making it impossible to commit mistakes in the work process. It is said that it is best to do things right the first time. It is even better to make it impossible to do it wrong the first time.

"It is very good to do anything right the very first time. It is even much better to make it impossible to do it wrong the first time."

When introducing Poka-Yoke in working systems, we need to keep a few principles in mind. These are summarized as follows:

a. The first and foremost objective is to achieve zero defects. It is not acceptable to produce any defect.

b. Mistake-proofing concepts are best originated from that person who is handling the machine and is the originator of the defect-free product—the worker. Therefore, it is of utmost importance to give respect to the worker. There is no second opinion.

Allow the worker to participate in the creative thinking process by undertaking some of the developmental activities and clearing out some of the mind-numbing repetitive tasks.

Here, we need to understand that to err is human. Machines do not make mistakes. We humans commit errors. Human errors are unintentional. These errors, in turn, cause inaccurate, damaged, or incomplete products

| Traditional view: Errors are inevitable | Modern view: Errors can be eliminated |
|---|---|
| • To err is human. | • While not all errors can be eliminated, many can be, or they can be reduced. |
| • Variation is natural and everywhere. | • Variation can be eliminated by different ways. |
| • More inspection can be beneficial. | • The need for inspection can be reduced or, in some cases, eliminated entirely. |

**FIGURE 8.1**
Traditional versus modern views on human errors.

that we define as defects. If a machine creates a defect, then we need to recheck the program that runs that machine. In this context, it would be interesting to note a few historical opinions about errors. These are enumerated in Figure 8.1.

Figure 8.1 essentially reasserts that although it is true that committing errors is human, in a manufacturing setup, errors can be largely reduced to a great extent, sometimes to zero. The ultimate goal is to eliminate defects by reducing or eliminating errors.

## The Poka-Yoke Techniques

There are a few well-researched and established error-proofing techniques. These are listed in Table 8.1. These techniques are classified into three types—warning, control, and shutdown. These all can be applied to the prevention of errors before their occurrence and to the detection of errors after their occurrence, so that defective parts do reach the next step in the manufacturing process.

Next, we will discuss and analyze the various Poke-Yoke, or mistake-proofing, techniques. The six most common techniques are (1) elimination, (2) replacement, (3) prevention, (4) facilitation, (5) detection, and (6) mitigation. These six techniques are explained in detail in the following sections.

**TABLE 8.1**

Techniques for Poka-Yoke or error proofing

| Technique | Prevention before Occurrence | Detection after Occurrence |
|---|---|---|
| • Warning | • Something is about to go wrong in the process. | • Immediately; as soon as something goes wrong |
| • Control | • Steps taken to control an occurrence. Errors do not occur. | • Nonconforming products cannot go on to the next stage and never can go to the customer. |
| • Shutdown | • When a mistake occurs. | • When the defect has already occurred. |

## Elimination

This technique brings the focus of the problem-solver toward eliminating the initial causal step in the entire process. If this particular process step is eliminated altogether from the process chain, the mistakes will not surface. This technique also refers to the removal of non-value-adding activities to make the process leaner. In a particular manufacturing setup, one may even redesign the product or the process in order to totally eliminate or to avoid recurring mistakes.

## Replacement

This technique deals with replacing the mistake-prone step with a more reliable one. In situations involving repetitive human motion, the process steps can be automated.

A typical example of this technique is the use of robots for repetitive work such as spray painting automotive parts, placement of parts on conveyors, and so on, for a variety of jobs.

## Prevention

In this technique, the product or process is modified or changed in such a way that even with a human error, the possibility of a mistake occurring is nil. In other words, there will be no possibility of human error. In typical cases, this technique may require adding a special attachment in order to accomplish these results.

Examples may include HDMI sockets for network connectors, a belt guard for a motor, a plastic safety guard inside an electrical plug, and so on.

## Facilitation

In this technique, the critical action steps are analyzed and evaluated as to whether or not the steps are absolutely necessary. In such cases, the steps are made comparatively easier so that making mistakes becomes more difficult. In other words, the possibility of mistakes occurring reduces drastically.

A few examples of such efforts include red-yellow-green traffic lights, colored insulation tapes, colored tags for cable identification in electrical wiring, and having a separate pedestrian path beside a motorway.

## Detection

Through this technique, a product or a process is modified so that when a mistake occurs or is about to occur an alarm goes off for initiating corrective actions. This can be accomplished using visual or electrical aids or even electronic attachments that indicate immediate attention is needed.

Typical examples may include infrared or laser light switches in cases of access breaches in a prohibited area, water level overflow indicators with visual or electric alarms, and so on.

### Mitigation

This last technique is designed so that in cases where mistakes occur even after all actions are taken, the results will be very minimal—so much so that, for all practical purposes, there may be no significant effect.

A few typical examples may include safety belts for working at great heights, an eraser for pencil marks, airbags in cars, lifeboats on ships, or even life jackets placed in airplanes.

### Poka-Yoke Devices

As discussed earlier, Poka-Yoke techniques are classified into three types. There are two types of devices that can be used to implement these techniques. They are (a) *control devices* and (b) *warning devices*. Control devices are used to eliminate the possibility of a mistake, whereas warning devices send a signal before or when a mistake occurs.

A typical example of a control device is an over-voltage protector that shuts down a parent machine in the case of a voltage surge. Similarly, an example of a warning device is the low fuel level indicator in an automobile.

The essence of these ideas is not to wait for any perfect solution but to act immediately by implementing the Poka-Yoke solutions as soon as possible and wherever applicable. In the case of industrial problem-solving, "doing it ASAP"[1]may have more importance than perfection, which will follow in any case.

---

## FMEA

The acronym FMEA stands for Failure Mode Effect Analysis, which is a standardized technique for understanding the challenges ahead when introducing a new product or process design, a new process step, or when implementing some changes. The concept of FMEA is quite old in industrial jargon, while the first formally documented FMEA was conducted early in the second half of the twentieth century. This is a structured technique used to identify and take care of fallout from potential failures due to foreseen or unforeseen problems so that preventive actions can be initiated to offset the results of an undesirable event [2]. Essentially, this is a technique to prevent

---

[1] ASAP = as soon as possible.

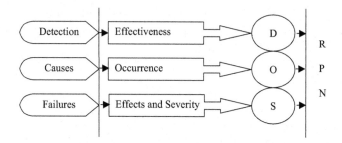

**FIGURE 8.2**
Elements of FMEA: failures, causes, and detection. S, O, and D stand for severity, occurrence, and detection, respectively.

problems. FMEA has very low risk; it is a very effective way to identify potential problems before they occur and to prevent them from occurring using whatever limited resources are available.

A FMEA analysis helps an industrial engineer quantify the risks associated with a new step and classify them according to severity (S), frequency of occurrence (O), and detection (D) based on similar experiences. There are three elements of an FMEA analysis. These are failures, causes, and detection. Failures have their effects and severity (S); causes have their frequency of occurrence (O); and detection has its effectiveness (D). These three elements of FMEA are detailed in Figure 8.2. For example, FMEA is similar to our practice of listening to a weather forecast before we leave for work. We try to get an idea and predict if the weather will require us to carry an umbrella, take mass transportation, or even use a personal car to avoid traffic on a busy road and reach the office on time. We try to anticipate and take actions accordingly, in order to achieve the desired results. When properly administered, this technique will help practitioners in diverse fields to proactively identify and reduce failures in existing and future processes.

### Types of FMEA Techniques

There are two types of FMEA techniques—process FMEA and FMEA design. While process FMEA is conducted predominantly in a manufacturing process, design FMEA is employed at the new product or process development stage. A quick look at the following will help us understand these two types of FMEA better.

#### *Process FMEA questions:*

- What are the potential failures, if the present process is followed?
- How can this manufacturing process or service fail to deliver its intended results?

### Design FMEA questions:

- How might this product design fail to yield the desired results?
- What are the potential avenues where the product will fail in its end use?

## Conducting an FMEA

The FMEA technique essentially has two fundamental aspects—*identifying* various modes of failure and *analyzing* their effects. There are standardized procedures for conducting the FMEA analysis in order to address potential failures and mitigate their effects.

Detection: Conducting a successful FMEA requires one to methodically follow a few steps. These steps are as follows.

Step 1: Identify potential failures and their corresponding effect. The *severity* (denoted as S) of the effect of the potential failures is assigned a number on a rating scale from one to ten.

Step 2: Evaluate the likelihood of occurrences (denoted as O) of the potential causes and assign a rating from one to ten.

Step 3: Evaluate the probability of detection (denoted as D) of the failure and assign a rating from one to ten.

Step 4: Calculate the risk priority number (RPN) by using the formula, $RPN = S \times O \times D$.

A quick look at the rating methodologies will help us understand the subject better. There are usually two types of rating systems. They are:

- Providing a rating of one to five, which is not very popular
- Providing a rating of one to ten, which is very popular

For these two scales, the guidelines detailed in Table 8.2 may be helpful for deciding on tentative ratings.

Step 5: List all the intended controls for reducing or preventing the occurrence of the root causes of the potential failures.

**TABLE 8.2**

Criterion for considering different FMEA ratings

| Rating | Detection | Occurrence | Severity |
|--------|-----------|------------|----------|
| 5 or 10 | No detection possible | Frequent | High |
| 1 | Effective | Rare | Low |

Step 6:  Based on the RPN results and the corresponding risks associated with these results, initiate actions after prioritizing the effective failure modes.

Step 7:  In case there are eventual changes in the product, process, and services, review and update the FMEA in order to understand the RPN results in a changed scenario.

### Reducing the Risk of Failure

There are various methodologies for reducing high RPNs in the FMEA process. During problem-solving, one of the tasks is to reduce the risk associated with potential failures in implementing the probable solutions. These risk-reducing methodologies can be summarized as follows.

- *Improve detection* of potential failures in the manufacturing process or in the delivery of services. If possible, provide a clear detection mechanism for a product before its usage by customers.
- *Reduce or eliminate the occurrence.*
- *Reduce the severity* of effects.

There must be very well-thought-out specific action plans when following all the aforementioned methodologies. In the next section, you will find a few critical examples to demonstrate some actions for reducing overall risk.

- Examples of actions to *reduce the severity* of effects from potential failures
  - Use of suitable personal protective equipment, such as welding glasses, helmets, gloves, and safety shoes while working in manufacturing process workshops
  - Providing front and rear bumpers in cars
- Examples of actions *to reduce the frequency* of potential failure occurrences
  - Effectively following a schedule of preventive maintenance
  - Using raw materials and spare parts with known and trustworthy supply origin.
  - Not changing various related processes frequently without thoroughly understanding the implications
  - Increasing the process capability of a manufacturing or service provision through statistical process control and proper experiment design.

- Examples of actions to *improve detection*
  - Online monitoring of all products being manufactured and services being provided through SCADA[2] or control charts
  - Calibration of all measuring devices and keeping a record of all calibration

## Stakeholder Analysis

When implementing a solution arrived at through a problem-solving journey, it will be of the utmost importance to analyze and understand the implications of solutions on different stakeholders in the product, process, or service chain. Stakeholders can be people, or even a group of people in department, who have a stake in the solution of the problem.

Stakeholder analysis usually is conducted for complex business decisions wherein there may be multiple groups of numerous stakeholders for every single decision. Though it is not expected that all the stakeholders will be satisfied by any one particular decision, the requirements of all the stakeholders should be noted before any decision is made. One important property of this technique is that it can work very well for both manufacturing and service industries.

In industrial problem-solving, we usually come across a variety of solutions. Often, there will be conflict among connected parties when arriving at acceptable solutions. Sometimes, in order to resolve an issue in one process stage, you may need to take some preventive actions during the prior process steps.

For example, the new actions may demand more work such as increasing the frequency of inspections. The people associated with that process stage may not be very interested in completing the extra work as envisaged. Though it may seem contrary to the principles of closely knit teamwork, it will be prudent on our part to accept that when we are dealing with teams, we essentially are dealing with emotional human beings.

On a systematic basis, stakeholder analysis can be conducted once—before the solutions are implemented—or on a regular basis—after the solutions are implemented, in order to understand the changing faces of time and demand.

---

[2] Supervisory control and data acquisition (SCADA) is a system of software and hardware elements that helps industrial organizations to generate data and provide data with preset analysis in a real time span.

## Real Problem-Solving

### A Whole Submersible Pump in Standby?

At the International Bus Body Building Company, a continuous process industry, engineers were facing a very simple but annoying problem of frequent failure in a costly fuel-lifting submersible oil pump. After thorough analysis of the problem, its history, and the possible solutions, the section responsible for the upkeep of the machines, the mechanical maintenance department, found that the pump's operation had become erratic. However, in the absence of a clear knowledge of the root cause of the problem, finding an immediate solution seemed too difficult.

The team then decided to keep one extra fuel pump in stock as a stand-by. This stand-by pump was a potential problem-solver in times of emergency. Though this solution of having an extra pump in stock was not the best one available to the team, the team decided to go ahead with this temporary solution. However, the extra cost of the pump would increase the cost of the inventory being maintained in the plant.

While doing a stakeholders analysis, during a routing meeting with all concerned, it was understood that the people in the stores department would be affected directly because, as a part of their performance appraisal, their yearly achievement-based incentive remuneration greatly depends on the cost of inventory. As a result, the officers in the stores department vehemently opposed the decision to have any extra pump in stock. So the user department decided to further analyze the problem of the faulty fuel pump and cancelled the extra inventory proposal.

Later, the team conducted a deep problem analysis, identified the root cause, and found that a faulty electrical junction was responsible for all the trouble. As a part of their routine job, mechanical maintenance department could resolve the issues without replacing the costly oil lifting pump thereby making this a justifiable solution.

This example shows how stakeholders may influence decision-making in the problem-solving journey.

## Network Diagram

A network diagram, as the name suggests, is a visual representation of the project schedule while working on problems and their solution. We often come across a similar situation where we need to work on the various steps systematically one after another. In order to make a few assumptions and predictions, it is helpful to visually depict the various steps, the interdependence of those steps, and the time difference that separates them. Network diagrams are helpful in understanding the time lines in a total problem-solving journey and the alternate paths that are available for us to follow. However, there are a few assumptions that should be made before such diagrams are prepared.

- The leader of the project is available as a resource and the required amount of support also is available.
- Most of the activities are well-known, and it would not be difficult to conduct necessary experiments and trials, if required.
- In addition to resources, network events in the problem-solving journey require active and creative thinking as well as logical hypotheses.
- Not much training is required when conducting the necessary trials for making the journey.

## Real Problem-Solving

### Timelines in Manufacturing Helical Pumps

At Star Dave Motors and Pumps Company, the helical pumps manufacturing unit has landed a prestigious order for supplying heavy duty rotary helical pumps. These pumps will be used for river-water pumping stations of the state-run irrigation department. Because of dwindling rainfall during the last three years, the groundwater level has gone down considerably and crop failures have become the order of the day. Therefore, the state is geared up to facilitate delivery to farms of water for irrigation by directly supplying from it from distant riverbed pumping stations.

Because of the crucial nature of the usage, the company chairman decides to direct all their resources toward increasing the production pace to meet the supply deadline. She asks her chief of the production staff to prepare the best possible process flowchart for supplying 25 such submersible pumps.

The production chief, Ms. Tirabasi, conducts a quick discussion session with her management team and prepares a process flow chart that shows the major work stages and the respective time duration that is required to complete the jobs in the various sections. Also, she makes a prediction for successfully meeting the supply deadline. The process flow chart is depicted in Figure 8.3.

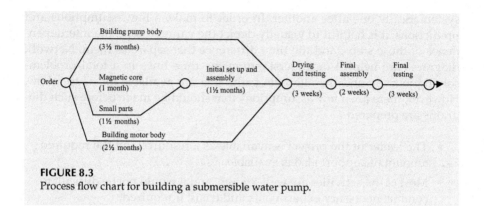

**FIGURE 8.3**
Process flow chart for building a submersible water pump.

A good Network diagram must be a clear, concise graphical representation. To clearly depict a sequence, it may be necessary to ask a few pertinent questions such as:

- What are the activities that precede or follow?
- What activities can occur concurrently?
- Where will the activities start and finish?

## A3 Documentation [3]

Before we discuss the A3 tool here, refer to the A3 Problem-Solving section in Chapter 2. There we have seen how the eight steps are followed in a very methodical and systematic manner. We also have seen the sectional deliverables of each steps. Here in this section, we will take note how on the method of documenting the results of each steps in a well designed format.

As discussed earlier, A3 thinking is an integral part of the Toyota Production System (TPS) which is discussed and popularized in several books, such as, *Understanding A3 Thinking [3], and* The Toyota Way [4]. In this section we will limit our discussion to the A3 format used for problem solving and underlining objectives for each entry. For better understanding of this problem-solving tool, we will look at two examples of A3 format. The first one directly follows the 8-step problem-solving approach. The second one displays a free flowing problem-solving story.

In Table 8.3, we find the standard A3 problem-solving process flow.

The A3 Problem-Solving template serves a few very important purposes:

a. It displays the entire problem-solving plan in one big page.

b. Since it displays graphs and pictorial data, it is very much visual.

c. The eight steps are written in such a way that the story unfolds from left hand top to right hand bottom following a two column reading.

**TABLE 8.3**

Format for A3 problem-solving

| A3 Number & Name | Team Members: | Overall Objectives |
|---|---|---|
| Tea Leader: | Stake Holders | Start Date & Planned Duration |
| 1. *Clarify the problem* | 4. *Analyse the root Cause* | 7. *Monitor results* |
| What is the problem? Who is interested in the problem? What benefit does solving this problem have for me? How does it help to address the goals of the business? | Clarify the root cause. Consider as many potential cause factors as possible through Interviews, - praetor charts, stratification, 5 whys, Cause and effects analysis, Process Capability Analysis etc | Monitor Results & send process findings to stakeholders. It may require more than one attempt to get the desired result. |

**A3 Problem-solving process flow 1**

| 2. *Breakdown the problem* | 5. *Develop countermeasure* | 8. *Standardise & Share Success* |
|---|---|---|
| What is the size of the problem? What data do I have? What are the component parts of this problem? | List as many potential countermeasures as possible. Identify an effective countermeasure that directly addresses the root cause. | Document the new process and set as new standard. Share the new standard through Horizontal deployment. |
| 3. *Set The target* | 6. *Implement counter measure* | |
| What outcome do I want? Visualise the desired results. Using the data, set a measurable and realistic goal. | Select the most practical and effective countermeasure(s). Create a clear and detailed action plan. Implement quickly. | |

    d. However, it would be further important to note again that what is important is not the template or the way it is designed, but the underlying concept behind it.

As you can well see that while the problem-solving is being done, a step by step story is unfolding in the A3 sheet of paper. As you go along, as you get new information or new modified data, you have to change the previous sections before you proceed further. Therefore, this A3 document remains a living document.

"There is no such thing as prefect A3, it is a living document and it gets improved at every step of new observation."

There is no such thing as prefect A3, every step you proceed you will get inspiration to improve the previous section. The idea here is to communicate all team members and bring consensus at every stage to move forward.

Since we will add a lot of information in one A3 sheet of paper, it is mandatory that we remain up-to-date, very concise and very precise. We will also add a lot of graphs and charts. Therefore, it is prudent to have the graphs and charts properly titled. Other important points are to ensure that a) the data represents actual scenario, b) the scale of the chart is consistent, and c) the targets are clear, visual and unambiguous.

## One Point Lesson (OPL)

One page summary reports can serve various purposes. After the problem-solving activity is completed, generally a detailed report is prepared. As discussed in the preceding section that A3 is a very effective way of reporting the entire problem-solving journey. In addition, for all problem-solving journeys, there can be a special learning that must be remembered and always kept in mind while performing any work related to that. This crucial learning which makes or breaks the entire situation can be documented and circulated to all stake holders so that they can take necessary actions when warranted. One such document can be this One Point Lesson (OPL).

During the problem-solving, while analyzing the situation and while standardizing and monitoring, you will come across some very important step in the standard work procedure, which, if not followed, may in all probability give rise to same problem again. Beside that an important step in a process may comprise of some key points. There will be obvious benefit of getting first- time-right results by following the key points in those important steps. This benefit of the key point and the important step in the whole process are to be highlighted and visually displayed in the One Point Lesson page. This learning is to be put into the minds of team members and taught specially for adherence. In Table 8.4, a format is presented to illustrate the concept.

After the problem-solving project was completed, the team identified a very important step in the process and a key point to adhere to so as to ensure that the returning glaze slip does not pick up air and entrap bubbles in the process. They documented these learning in a One Point Lesson format as detailed in Table 8.4.

As you see in this Table that the benefits, key points and the important steps are written in one page for very easy access for all. Moreover, observe that there are two persons who are directly involved in maintaining the process parameters have understood and witnessed respectively. This step ensures that the real stake holders are engaged and are part of the real problem-solving story.

**TABLE 8.4**

One point lesson

<table>
<tr><th colspan="5">One Point Lesson</th></tr>
<tr><td># OPL</td><td>17/2010</td><td>Prepared By<br>Signature:</td><td>Date</td><td>26/07/2010</td></tr>
<tr><td>OPL Type</td><td>Process</td><td>Approved By<br>Signature:</td><td>Date</td><td>27/07/2010</td></tr>
<tr><td>Section</td><td>Glaze spraying</td><td colspan="2">Department</td><td>Glazing</td></tr>
<tr><td>Important Step:</td><td colspan="4">Maintain the glaze viscosity at 60-65 sec (B4 Ford cup), and never below 55 sec.</td></tr>
<tr><td>Key Points:</td><td colspan="4">Maintain the overflow glaze return in such a way that the width of the flow from the pipe must not be greater that width of a thumbnail.<br><br>Level of the glaze stock in the re-circulating tank must not be more than 6 inches below the sieve mounted on the tank. This is to maintain the glaze fall height below 6 inches.</td></tr>
<tr><td>Benefits:</td><td colspan="4">If the viscosity is on the higher side and return flow is less, then the chance of air bubble entrapment reduces drastically. This resolves the face hole problem in flat ware.</td></tr>
</table>

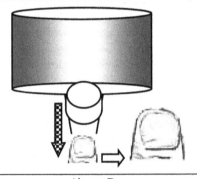

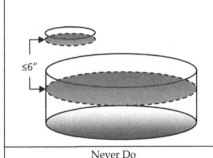

| Always Do | Never Do |
|---|---|
| Always keep the width of the glaze flow lesser than thumb size. | Never allow the glaze level in the tank to fall more than 6 inches below the sieve holder. |

| Understood by: | Witnessed by: |
|---|---|

## Real Problem-Solving

### Bubbles Resulting in Holes on the Face

Glazed flatwares are produced following a standard ceramic manufacturing process that consists of raw material batch preparation, spray-drying, pressing, glazing, firing and selection. In this production process, one of the important process steps is to coat the green ware with a homogenous glaze slip (mixture of chosen ground inorganic and inorganic raw materials in water suspension) with a pre-defined coating thickness of 0.7 to 1.1 mm. This will produce the impervious glassy layer on the usable side. The coating process requires the flat ware to travel on a belt conveyor under a glaze-slip curtain fall.

The flat-ware picks up the required amount (measured in coating thickness) of the glaze by travelling through the glaze curtain at a particular speed. The other related parameters of this process are; surface temperature of the green (unfired) flatware, density (g/cc), and viscosity (flow-rate through a B4 Ford cup) of the glaze slip. If these parameters are not followed as per the process specification, different glaze defects appear, such as, thin glaze, surface waviness, dimples, pin holes, face holes, edge crack, and glaze peel etc. If any defects arise which is more than the usual process limits (common cause variations), it is usual practice to first check and rectify any parameters that are out of specification.

In one such case, during many a months of manufacturing, it was observed that the defect occurrence (%) of a particular defect 'face-hole' has been very high. This was sometime as high as 15% in some days. The products with even one face-hole in it would be classified as of inferior (factory seconds) quality and are sold at much lower price. The process quality assurance team did a thorough Gemba walk, analyzed the entire process, its parameters, and their inter-relationships. However, they could not get any root cause that could be a potential reason for the defects to appear. Later, the team started to look for parameters and process situations that are beyond the scope of normal measurements and beyond the prior knowledge base of the manufacturing art. After many observations, hypothesis, experiments and validation trials, it was concluded that if the viscosity of the glaze slip is on the lower side of the operating limit and the stock level of the glaze slip is below a certain limit, the overflow glaze slip, while returning back to the day tank stock, picks up air and entrap that in the glaze. The glaze slip is of viscous nature and remains continuously under stirring in order to keep the raw materials in suspension. Therefore, the entrapped air remains entrapped as a cluster of hundreds of small bubbles and circulate in the entire process of glazing operation. These bubbles also remain in the glaze when the later is applied on the flat-ware. Thereafter, the bubbles burst and leave a so called face holes on the surface. Later, when these observations were considered, corrective actions were taken, the defects drastically got reduced to maximum 1.5% on a long term basis.

## Review Questions

1. Explain the various considerations for implementing a Poka-Yoke solution.
2. Give an everyday example for all types of Poka-Yoke techniques discussed in this chapter.
3. How are the severity ranking, occurrence ranking and detection rankings are given for a process FMEA. Illustrate with example.
4. How does the customization of rankings help you arrive at better overall FMEA results?
5. Critically think and illustrate the merits and demerits of a stake holder analysis.
6. Illustrate with example, how a network diagram can help you visualize the various processes.
7. Explain in detail the A3 problem-solving reporting process. Explain how A3 report necessarily and sufficiently address the various sections of a structured problem-solving process?
8. Discuss the significance of the One-Point–Learning concept.

## References

1. Smith, Gerald F. *Quality Problem-solving*. Milwaukee: ASQ Quality Press, 1998.
2. "Procedure for Failure Mode, Effects and Criticality Analysis (FMECA)." RA–006–013–1A. Washington, DC: National Aeronautics and Space Administration, 1966. Retrieved 2010-03-13.
3. Sobek, Durward K. and Smalley, Art. *Understanding A3 Thinking: A Critical Component of Toyota's PDCA Management System*. Boca Raton, FL: CRC Press/ Productivity Press, 2008.
4. Jeffrey K. Liker, *The Toyota Way: 14 Management Principles from the World's Greatest Manufacturer*, McGraw-Hill, New York, 2004.

WHEN GOWRIE MET KRISHNA:

*Gowrie:* I have a short-term solution for one of your long-term problem.

*Krishna:* That's okay. But I would rather prefer a long-term solution to a short-term problem.

*Gowrie:* That's for sure! Where there is a will, there is a way. Where there is a problem, there is a solution.

*Krishna:* Don't be so over-whelmed or so over confident. Nor you should be so clever that you ignore the most obvious.

*Gowrie:* If I can't solve it, better run fast!

*Krishna:* Oh, no! Running away from the problem will only increase the distance from solution. The easiest way to escape from the problem is to solve it!

# Appendix: Critical Thinking

While trying to understand the various methods of problem-solving in a real-life scenario, at every step, we will encounter an array of noisy situations wherein we must think, reflect, and make decisions in order to move forward. This process requires special skill and ability to navigate and correlate between ambiguous circumstances to decipher complex situations. These skills are part of critical thinking abilities. In fact, these critical thinking skills are another set of tools that one uses in achieving problem-solving goals. These skills listed here are detailed in the following sections. Some pertinent critical thinking exercises are also included in order to trigger thoughts in your mind in this direction.

The five most important critical thinking skills are:

1. Interpretation
2. Analysis
3. Inference
4. Evaluation
5. Explanation

We will discuss all these critical thinking skills in the following sections.

## Interpretation

Interpretation is the action of explaining the meaning of something. This act may include elucidation, explanation, and exposition among many other similar meanings. This skill describes the ability to understand different data and present those to people using clear and easy to understand terminology.

Throughout the entire problem-solving journey, one will receive data that will come from a variety of sources. Usually, these contain units that are as varied as the sources themselves may be. This skill of interpretation will help one to understand and communicate the concepts to fellow team members. This, in turn, will help in determining a further course of action.

One of the major ways to master this skill is to recognize its importance and gravity. A mere consciousness of this skill for interpretation will help one improve in this skill, as one will always try to undertake a better interpretation.

### CRITICAL THINKING EXERCISES

A man goes to a grocery shop and asks for a bottle of wine. Imagine the facial expression of the shopkeeper when he is replying to the customer and interpret.

Imagine a deserving classmate does not find his name on the list of students promoted to the next level class. Try to visualize the facial expression of this student and try to interpret the meaning behind it.

Another great way of mastering this skill is to take a few everyday examples and use interpretation. While doing this, remember to think deeply about the concept and try to improve as much as possible.

## Analysis

Analysis is a detailed examination of the elements or structures of something. This can include investigation, inspection also. This is the process of separating something into its constituent elements, the roots. Analytical skill describes the ability to assimilate various data (that are scattered and from various sources) and connect them in a single thread in order to further understand the story they represent. This skill is used when making a detailed examination.

While the term "interpretation" refers to understanding and communicating, "analysis" refers to finding the meaning.

Mastering this skill provides one with the ability to "read between the lines" and find the intended meaning from expressed data points.

### CRITICAL THINKING EXERCISE

Imagine that you are discussing a few common issues with your colleague. During discussion among many other topics the following statements came for review. Analyze and try to determine whether the following statements appear to be an opinion or a fact. Further analyze the statements and make a 5-why analysis to find out the root cause of the problem reported in the statements.

a. Smoking is injurious to health.

b. My telephone number is very difficult to remember.

## CRITICAL THINKING EXERCISE

Roup arrives at home around 8:20 pm and finds that lights are off. Can Roup infer that her mother is not yet home from her office?

Moulin goes for a week's off from the hectic office schedule. After the vacation, she comes back with darker skin that looks like usual sunburn. Can her friend Julia infer that Moulin was at the beach some 90 miles away?

On a cloudy day, while en route to your office, you observe that some people carry umbrella with them. Can you infer that there was weather forecast on radio that predicted showers?

## Inference

The meaning of the word refers to the act or process of inferring: such as the act of passing one proposition or judgment considered as true to another whose truth is believed to follow from that of the former. Inference is a conclusion reached on the basis of evidence and reasoning. Inferences are based on information provided as well as from personal experience which may relate to the problem being discussed. Sometimes making inferences may mean making a reasoned guess with the aid of prior knowledge and predictions. In problem-solving, we will deal with a big set of data. Analyzing those data will help us draw inferences.

This skill provides one with the ability of identifying various elements to create a hypothesis for solving a problem using the available data at hand.

When using this skill, we try to extrapolate data and data analysis to find the final objective.

Good training in this skill can be obtained by analyzing the balance sheet of an organization as well as practicing comprehension of a passage containing a set of data. We can use observation and background knowledge together with some known assumptions to make sensible conclusions!

## Evaluation

Evaluation is the making of a judgment or assessment about the amount, number or value of something. This skill helps in understanding the credibility of a statement, the comments of a person about an experience, and in determining an individual's understanding of a particular incident.

## CRITICAL THINKING EXERCISE

Imagine you are entrusted with leading a problem-solving group and you are conducting a brainstorming session to find the root cause of a problem. Your team members have various backgrounds and are comprised of doctors, MBAs, and even workers from the shop floor. As the team's leader, you are responsible for bringing out the best in the team. You must understand concepts and be able to explain them clearly and concisely. Therefore, the first thing you will want to do is to evaluate the situation at hand. However, this evaluation should take place after you have skillfully interpreted, analyzed, and inferred concepts from a given set of data. This evaluation requires you to think about the gravity of the present situation and the probable solution vis-à-vis the probable outcomes based upon your actions. This skill of evaluation helps you understand the reaction, response, and repercussions of your steps. Evaluation will also help you foresee and forecast what may happen. This is very crucial as you think about possible outcomes. If they seem unworthy or counterproductive, you may well abandon those actions. An evaluation exercise helps you change your course of action before you actually take any action.

In problem-solving, during various opinion forums this skill of evaluating will help the team make judgment to take or reject the opinions or the data in questions.

## Explanation

With this skill, you will not only be able to understand concepts yourself, but you also will be able to restate, paraphrase, and elaborate on the meaning of the input data or statements. You will be able to further elaborate on the inherent meaning of the input.

In a real-life scenario, most working teams are comprised of members with varied backgrounds, qualifications, and experience. The team members may not be as well-versed as you are in a particular subject. As the person in charge, you should be able to add an explanation about a concept under discussion.

Imagine you want to explain how a diesel engine runs to two persons of different backgrounds; one is a member of the human resources department and the other is a psychology professor at a university. The two individuals differ in their knowledge, experience, and perspectives on life. Would your

## CRITICAL THINKING EXERCISE

Imagine you have volunteered to teach to fourth graders in a middle school which is located in a very hot and sunny climatic zone for the most of the year. The temperature remains very cool and really enjoyable in the morning and in the evening time. The students generally enjoy very gayful time during the early morning before sunrise and afternoon till evening. However, the students never experienced the beauty of a snow clad mountain base. Also they do not have any idea of winter sports.

How would you explain to the students why the sky is blue in general or appears red in the morning or evening.

How would you explain the phenomenon of why the rainfall usually increases during a thunderstorm to a group of high school students?

How would you explain about a snow sport like sledging or ice-skating?

explanation be same for both of them? For both individuals to have a similar understanding of the concepts involved, you will need to provide an explanation in a language that is comprehensible to both of them. Your explanations may vary if you need explain to both of them together or separately.

# *Index*

Printed in the United States
by Baker & Taylor Publisher Services